For

Angus and Anita Brown

I am so happy for you to have a copy of The National Hotel. Here's hoping that you will get pleasure from reading my family's memoirs. Best wishes —

Ruth Lemming

THE

NATIONAL

HOTEL

by

Ruth Rucker Lemming

This Book Is For
My Daughter
My Nieces and Nephew
and
Great-Nieces and Great-Nephews
With Love

The materials in this book were compiled from:
Remembrances
Personal Interviews
Tape Recordings
Letters
Diaries

My especial gratitude to:
Jewel Gibson for her help with manuscript
Sylvia Corolla for her help with typing
Evelyn Mann and Ready Writers

This is a true story of the National Hotel of Franklin, Texas and of my Mother's life there for thirty-five years. During the heyday of the small town hotel, Minnie reared her three children and assisted with her five grandchildren. The hotel changed through the years, but its influence on all of us was indelible — almost as lasting as the force of Mama's personality — as sturdy as an oak.

I was there all the time, sometimes sharing Mama's confidences, but more often just listening to her and watching her. But the hub of our family was the National Hotel. These are the remembrances.

THE OLD HOTEL

THE NEW HOTEL

TABLE OF CONTENTS

MAMA

I

"To strive, to seek, to find and not to yield."

— *Alfred Lord Tennyson*

With Emphasis on Minnie Lee Holton Weeden Rucker. Called Mrs. Minnie Rucker, Minnie, or Mama.

I remember Mama. Mama sitting placidly in her rocking chair behind the hotel's registration desk in the office of the National Hotel. Usually she was quilting, for her hands, like her brain, were never idle. Occasionally she would stand and straighten the only picture on the wall — the picture of her late husband, Henry Rucker, as he took the oath of office as County Clerk of Robertson County.

My little chair was close beside Minnie's, as people who knew her well called her. I wondered about the man in the picture whom I would have called Papa had he not died so tragically when I was an infant. I could almost read Mama's thoughts because she always confided in me. Just now it seemed, she was hearing her late husband's friends proffering advice. "Now Minnie, I know that Henry would not want his money to be used to buy a hotel." Another had said, "You know how the world looks at it: Only a loose woman would run a hotel." But she had been encouraged by Mr. Abe Silverman's counsel: "A voman vould be a goot manager for the hotel vere I make my home."

This particular night it was about 8:30 of an early May evening in 1907, just three years after we had moved to the hotel. I had been told the story of that move often enough. There Mama had stood with her little brood of three children and one old man looking at the hotel which was to be her home for thirty-five years.

Jimmie, just out of her one year at college, gave a look

1

around as she took me, her baby sister, in her arms to relieve Mama. Robert, my older brother, peered into every nook and corner, seeking the features that would be either work or fun. Off to one side, the old man, Minnie's father, Thomas Courtney Holton, standing solitary and subdued, observed also. He didn't know whether he actually belonged here, since Henry Rucker's money was to be used for the first payment. But his daughter, Minnie, had always been dutiful and kind. She had "honored her father", as the Bible taught. Besides, he didn't have any other place to go; so he surveyed the hotel with interest, trying to see what he could do to occupy his time.

Minnie could see that the walls needed papering; the floors needed covering; the steps needed repairing; the entire place was wearing a dilapidated and desolate air. Well, she knew who could make things better; and there wasn't a lazy bone in her body. The dirt and desolation would soon disappear with a little Bon Ami, fresh clean beds, and window curtains. Hard work and stick-to-it-iveness would make a great change, and might help her forget her sorrows as well.

She stood for a moment, silently, in memory of her dear, dead husband and to gather up her courage. Then Minnie grabbed the well-packed suitcases, the boxes which held clothes and cooking utensils, and the few treasures of pictures, phonograph records, and vases — motioning to the two older children to help carry these treasures. Then she squared her shoulders, set her jaw, pressed her lips together, pulled her skirt down, held her head high, fixed her eyes forward and marched down the long porch and into the National Hotel office. The three children followed close behind: I, Baby Ruth, still in Jimmie's arms, Robert continually searching out new things. The old man brought up the rear, catching something of his daughter's spirit of determination as she tramped into the lobby of the National Hotel for the first time.

Mama rocked contentedly there behind the desk and went on with her story: "I wonder what those men would say now, Ruthie — just three years later — now that I am the first female member of the Franklin Chamber of Commerce. Me, just on the

2

shady side of forty." She smoothed an unruly lock of hair as a smile played around the corners of her mouth.

As she talked, Mama's hands worked avidly on the Oak Leaf and Acron quilt spread out on the chairs beside her. "Ruthie, you didn't sleep well last night, did you? I heard you trying to jabber to your grandfather across the hall. Now, he's getting old, baby. You must let him sleep."

"I just wanted to ask him about my brother, Bob," I answered. "I miss him so much since he left us to go to Kansas."

At the mention of Bob's name, Mama would either stop quilting or jab her finger with a needle. "Don't worry about Bob. He'll take care, and he'll be home before we know it."

"But why did he run away?"

"Some things you aren't old enough to discuss, Ruthie. It's your bed-time now. Run on, and I'll come in a few minutes to kiss you goodnight."

Determinedly, she pulled her mind back to the quilt in front of her — held rigidly to the pattern by each stuffed acorn, by the tracery of the oak leaves into the symmetry of the whole.

She loved this time of day — when all of her duties as a small town hotel owner and manager were over, and it was not yet time to go to bed because she hoped for the arrival of some late overnight guests with their touches of outside life and excitement.

Dimly Minnie heard the muffled hum of the drummer's voices. They were sitting at the round black oilcloth covered domino table in front of the bay window, lighted by an electric drop light, covered with a hanging green shade. Their usual half mocking patter was about Abe Silverman and his little black rule book on dominoes (a rule book for a man who could not read a word).

Occasionally, one of the men would wander past the two wash basins with the towel rack above them to the water cooler in the corner for a drink from the communal tin cup. Then she heard one of the drummers declare: "Well, I'll bid eighty-four."

Mr. Silverman rubbed his hands together and ejaculated vociferously, "Gentlemen, you bought a mule." I could hear the murmur of their voices, too. They had almost lulled me to sleep when Mama came to kiss me goodnight.

The next morning grandpa took me for our usual morning walk. We must have made quite a picture touring the long front and back porches. I, pushing my way in a froglike motion with legs too long for the baby walker; the old man tottered beside with saddened features, brightening only when his gaze focused on me. I can still remember his face and how he moved about nervously when he asked, "Why does the good Lord see fit to keep me in this vale of tears?" His mind seemed to wander. "Would that I might go to the arms of my beloved wife! Ah, she was so beautfiul; I adored her black hair and eyes," and he went on to tell about their marriage in old Decatur County, Georgia.

Then he changed his manner. "Come along, Ruthie. It's time for my hot toddy that the doctor prescribed. I like it better when you have the first spoonful from the top of the glass." So for four years — until his death — I had a teaspoon full of hot toddy every morning.

He pushed the baby walker into the door of the kitchen. (More than seventy years later, I can still feel its welcoming warmth.) "Mrs. Morgan, will you be so kind as to prepare my hot toddy now?" The Mrs. Morgan he referred to was the cook at the hotel who originally came from Poland. She wore a rounded cap with lace ruching on her head. Her hair was done up under the cap so none of it would escape and get in the food.

I remember the other rooms, of course, but the kitchen was the most interesting in the whole house — Morgan's domain — indeed, the hub of the hotel. A large black cookstove covered almost all of one side of the room. The roaring fire in its giant belly was frequently replenished with sticks of stovewood from the great woodbox beside it, the box which everyone who came in from the backyard was supposed to replenish in turn — summer and winter alike. Morgan allowed no one to sit on the little stool beside it except me. She always had a kind word for me, a

4

pat on the head and a shoulder for my tears as I grew up.

How often I was to wish I had taken advantage of the opportunity to become bilingual. How well I remember Morgan's expansive figure flipping out the back door, shaking her coat tail, and muttering, "Shalum ne duper tach nea." I have no more idea now than then of her meaning.

But Morgan's words and expressions were to become a permanent part of my vocabulary: "My rose was bud out but soon was cut down." "Right's right and wrong's wrong, and right don't wrong nobody." "Did you go all the way to New Baden to get this many dirty dishes?"

Morgan told me fascinating tales. She said, "Now set down here, honey, and I'll tell you about working my way over on a boat from the old country. Ruthie, I never had on a pair of shoes until I was grown. In New York I met and married Henry Morgan, who was a carpenter and house painter. We come to live in Franklin, Texas because there was work in the town. I'll have you know that my home across the tracks is as neat as a pin. Flowers blossom in my hand-dug underground greenhouse all winter long, and my daughters have been raised to be as respectable as the next one."

But Mama, Mrs. Minnie Rucker, for whom she was to cook in the National Hotel for more than twenty years, was her real ideal, her mentor. Morgan said, "I have no idea how old I am nor my actual birthday; so I will just adopt your age as my own, and we will each proudly wear a rose from my greenhouse as a gift for our mutual birthday on January the first."

Their fusses were frequently interspersed with much muttering and shaking of coat tails; but Mama was apt to sit on the high stool ever so often and share comforting confidences and a bowl of Morgan's incomparable soup from the soup kettle which was always on the back of the stove, a mute reminder of her oft-repeated claim: "I can make good soup if I have the greements."

The hotel was Mama's refuge; even though she left, she always came back. Morgan took care of the kids when Mama was busy or had gone somewhere. Morgan always had a favorite child—first Ruth, then a later child—and baked a little cake or roll for her. There were no telephones in Franklin in those days. Every morning a clerk from each grocery store would come to the hotel and take the order for the day; then go back and fill it; then deliver it to the back door. One clerk drove a red wagon pulled by two little mules because no one had cars then. Later, when there were telephones, Mama had only to phone Gilland Brother's store and say, "I want a can of peas, Harry," and he would run down the back way with it—to be met by me. Mama never had to identify herself. Her voice was very distinctive.

I sat on the stool in the corner, as was my habit when there weren't many people eating in the dining room and I could see, on the opposite side from the stove, a long table containing wash pans and drying racks for the dirty dishes brought in from the dining room. There was the middle table where Minnie was wont to sit, called the serving table. My favorites were the desserts and salads on a little table to one side just under a homemade cabinet for clean dishes. One of the most intriguing sights was a big rat-trap always in a prominent place on the floor. Oh — everything was shipshape in Minnie's — that is Morgan's — kitchen.

Just behind the stove I could see a walk-through pantry connecting with the family rooms; and outside the back door was the original pantry, now converted into an ironing room. "This," said Mrs. Hattie Andrews, our cleaning maid, "is my domain." If she were to list her duties, she might say, "I stand and iron endlessly on stacks of white tablecloths and napkins, and on sheets and pillow cases and sometimes on Ruth's dresses. I try to be ready to go upstairs to clean the room after a guest checks out, but the flat irons are always hot on the back of the kitchen stove; and look high, Ruth, all around the one little window the washtubs hang on their pegs."

Just outside, I could see the wash yard, Aunt Fanny's kingdom. As she put it, "I has all sorts of dryin' lines and a big black wash pot." (The pot which was to sit just outside Ruth's apartment containing a beautiful flowering fern—so many years later.) "I pokes the clothes a-bubblin' in the pot. Then I rinses them in tin wash tubs and hangs 'em out to dry in the sun."

Aunt Fanny was an ancient, very black woman who had

been a slavery Negro — full of many enchanting tales. She stated: "I done been sold from Alabama to a Texas owner and I shorely does recollect when the stars fell on Alabama. Further mo, my weddin' to my husband, who y'all calls Uncle Otter, was jus' tip top, and we will think about it all our days. We didn't do no modern weddin'. We jus' jumped over a broomstick." Oh, she entertained all of us with numerous tales.

There were big bois d'arc trees in the backyard and hackberry trees in the front yard. I used to pop the hackberries with my shoes on the sidewalk. A cistern in the back side yard was the place from which I loved to draw water with a pulley. Nearby was the Texas Star flower bed Mama had made from plants and flowers surrounded by Pink Radiance roses — looking like a giant quilt spread open for the world to see. She had planted a gorgeous American Beauty rose in the center of the star. Around it were fragrant tube roses. Tiny snowdrops drooped their heads in its border. This flower garden was the pride and joy of Mama's life.

Several different people returned to the hotel again and again during the years. They seemed almost like members of the family. For example, Dr. Ellis of the University of Texas conducted experiments on land nearby. Mr. and Mrs. Schoenburg, a retired couple from Wisconsin, came every year. They were so fascinated with Mama's far-sighted plans drawn for a new hotel that they loaned her money to build a brick hotel on the spot where the old frame one had stood. Mr. Michael Lime, a geologist, died at the hotel, leaving a little carved monkey which could see, hear or speak no evil. I have that monkey; I keep it. Every time I look at it, I think about Mama — whom I can hear saying, "That's good advice. Listen to that little monkey!" Mrs. Rucker considered the boarders her family, so she felt justified in eavesdropping on whatever they said. Miss Masterson, Miss Axtell, who gave me a little handpainted tea set, Mr. Will Coffield, Mr. Edmundson, Judge Lane from Hearne — all and many more came over and over again.

Judge Lane came rushing in late one afternoon explaining volubly, "I want to check out. I won't be able to spend the night with you, Mrs. Rucker.'' Realizing too late what he had said, he blundered on, "Oh, but you don't understand. I have a ride to Hearne, and I won't be able to sleep with you tonight.'' Mama was never allowed to live this incident down.

A young man, a former Franklin resident, came to the hotel every two or three years with a crew of girls selling magazines. They were always noisy, and were quite popular with the local male citizenry. One morning at two a.m. Minnie had had all of it she could stand; so she stalked up the stairs calling out: "You will have to get these girls out of my house right now, this instant. Not only have I nor my other guests slept a wing, but when two of Franklin's leading drunks try to slip up the back stairs, that is enough.''

In those days before school buses, Mama was responsible for several country boys getting to go to high school by working at the hotel for room and board. She made them realize the value of an education and saw to it that they studied. A great love for education was one of Mama's predominant characteristics; she wanted everyone to get as much education as possible. This had started when her mother slipped and fell on the step of a surrey and broke her hip. Always college had remained there, peeping over Minnie's shoulder. She had wanted Jimmie to go to college. Jimmie had wanted her own children to go. Mama wanted me to go. My daughter, Jean, must go. To Minnie, Robert, and their children, there was no other way of life than going to college. I think Mama's granddaughter, Minnie, pleased her more than any of the rest of us because she was valedictorian of Franklin High School the year she graduated.

I remember, especially, Sam Sanders who just sailed over the iron fence surrounding the front yard, not deigning to open the gate. But Hollis Frazier took the cake. One day a couple of ladies came in from a parked car and asked if they could go to the restroom. Hollis looked at them with a puzzled expression for a minute and then escorted them to the parlor door saying, "You can rest in there. Mrs. Rucker won't care.''

Those were the days of outdoor toilets. *The Ladies Toilet*

for the National Hotel, a four-holer, was inside the back fence, so it was not locked. Nearby, but separated, with its entrance outside the fence, was *The Men's Toilet*. This building always fascinated me for I was not allowed ever to enter it. The key to the outside john hung on the first post in the office. Mr. Silverman would take the key down and stay for what seemed an inordinately long time in the men's john. One day I sneaked the key and looked at the place. There was nothing very strange about it save the trough-like looking thing just inside, the huge signs advertising medicine for gonorrhea and gleet, and the four letter words written all over the walls which I was not permitted to use, but which I later read in Ginsberg's poetry.

Mr. Silverman was our permanent guest. To Mama, he seemed to belong. To me, Mr. Abe Silverman was the only man always in my life. His room was upstairs at the head of the stairway. It contained the most beautiful wash stand I had ever seen, with two little high marble shelves on each side. There was a bowl and pitcher in each room, and a tall Betsy; but there was just one bathroom and one toilet on each floor — even in the later rebuilt hotel.

I often heard Mr. Silverman's stories about how he had started his business career with a pack on his back. Going through the country, he would peddle his novelties and necessities; later he had a general mercantile business in Franklin and a jewelry store and several other buildings in Waco. Mr. Silverman never married but had brought numerous brothers and sisters and nieces and nephews from the old country to the United States. They lived in Hearne, Texas and New York City — both of which seemed far away to me. He was decidedly civic-minded, gave the money for a sidewalk to be placed all around the new school building, and was on every committee for the good of the town, and was such a good domino player that men would drive for miles to play by his rules.

Every night at supper, where the people had a boarding house reach for the sausage and smoked ham, Mr. Abe would watch the biscuit plate carefully until someone took the last biscuit. Then he would rub his hands together exultingly, gloatingly, and pounce: "Just enuff beeskits!" On other occasions he would rub his hands together pleasurably and contentedly: "Mrs. Rucker, there are nine things you serve to eat that I like. All of 'ems hash."

At meal time, Robert would go through his little spiel about "What will you have to drink? Buttermilk, sweetmilk, iced tea, hot tea, coffeeeeeeee" — drawling it out and almost making a song of it. Then — "What kinda pie will you have? Coconut, pecan, chocolate?" There was always a choice from soup to nuts, and he always saved a little sliver of pie for me.

But Mr. Abe was especially attentive to me. Frequently, he would take me on his knee and come out with "Molly Bailey's circus is coming to town. Ain't that wonnerful? They got fourteen elephants. Why-y-y-y-y, Rut, your eyes are as big as saucers."

One habit of Mr. Abe's which I will never forget was his usual custom on Christmas Eve. He would come down the street from Gilland Brother's Store with a cheery grin on his face, crying out, "Creesmus gift! Creesmus gift!" Then he would hand each member of the family a small, square package. We did not need to open them. Year after year they contained the same gift; a ladies white handkerchief with a small colored flower embroidered in the corner. I don't think anyone ever thought of saying "Happy Hanukkah!" to him.

Mama looked at me refectively. "You know, Ruthie, you make me think of your sister Jimmie when she was a little girl. (She often said this when my stool would be out of place in the kitchen.) Your father, Henry, was extremely bashful. It was hard on him to come courting me. He always wore a black hat in those days, which he would place on the hall tree just inside the front door. Jimmie was a very orderly child, and she would take his hat, march over to the big man who was later to become her stepfather and put it determinedly in his hands—every time he came."

Then her mind would wander even farther back and she would tell me stories of her own childhood. "I know you can't imagine, Ruth, what it was like to be the youngest daughter in a family of thirteen children. I'm sure I was spoiled rotten as I played around happily, usually with my dog for a companion. My father idolized me; one of the ways he showed it was to make me his companion on our annual shopping spree to Kosse. We raised nearly all our food on the farm, and my mother and sisters canned or dried food all year long. But there were some things we had to buy such as sugar, rice, flour, baking powder, soda, fresh fruits, and — best of all — material for making clothes, even though the tow sacks for other products were always utilized for aprons, quilt tops, and dish towels. But I always got to select the bolts of material for making our dresses and the boys' shirts and underwear. You may be sure, Ruth, that they were very colorful and eye-stopping.

"And guess what, dear; I got to spend the night in the wagon yard with my father. That *might* have been the first time that I got to stay in a hotel, but Papa and I would just sleep in the back of the wagon, cuddled under my mother's handmade quilts. The noises would keep me awake for some time, but after awhile I'd fall asleep and dream contentedly of our wagon loaded and ready to go, and of Old John pulling us over the long, lonely miles through rolling hills beneath the cloudless sky of a Texas golden autumn."

Mama's thoughts flew from subject to subject like a butterfly flitting from flower to flower. She picked up a picture of my younger brother who had died before I was born, and looked at it sadly. I, Ruth, called him "Little Duffey", since he had died at the age of four months and so would always remain "Little Duffey."

Mama's hands were best kept busy piecing quilts. Sometimes she made one a night — probably more than one thousand altogether. The best one, I thought, was the *Oak Leaf and Acorn*. Each oak leaf and acorn was stuffed separately to give the whole a three dimensional and sculptured look. She made one for me, but after she had the chance to sell it, she made me another. The stitches are not so perfect and some of the material is faded, but the quilt hidden away in my cedar chest is still beautiful.

When Mama was really in a lonely mood, she'd work all night. The cares of the day seemingly would just slip away when she made a *Friendship Quilt*. All the friends of the recipient would embroider their names on prepared blocks. Then Mama would put them together and quilt them with intricate patterns. She made a quilt for each new bride in the family; she also made one for each new baby; in fact, she would start on one just as soon as a relative was pregnant.

Mama was never satisfied with a plain pattern. She'd buy all sorts of patterns and combine and change them — often making up completely new ones. She made one called the *Star of Russia,* one called *Double Star,* and one *Lily of the Valley.* She quilted them in shell designs. One special design was called *The Chambered Nautilus.* She sent a *Star of Texas* as a gift to F. D. Roosevelt in the White House; Mama treasured the letter of thanks she received signed "Eleanor."

She made many for rooms in the hotel. They saved money, and supplied warm cover. She worked on them for the need of it, for she was never more relaxed than when she was making a quilt. But during the last few years in the hotel, her eyes were bad; so she turned to crocheting and knitting and embroidery. Her innate talent for making things was shown by using larger needles, making geometric designs on the sewing machine and appliqueing flowers on unbleached domestic. She set up a quilting frame in my room when I went to college because it had the space for a 20-foot frame. Making quilts and all the other handwork satisfied a basic desire in her nature — the creation of Beauty.

A really red letter day in Mama's life was the one on which she sold the *Oak Leaf and Acorn* quilt to a drummer for the unheard sum of fifty dollars. She laid hands on the money and took Jimmie, her niece Alys Truett, Miss Kitty Davlin, and me to Galveston for a weekend. She had to make bathing suits, complete with sleeves and bloomers, for us all.

Mama was a real seamstress. I have seen her cut out a dress for Little Minnie after two p.m., prepare and serve supper in between, and have an attractive garment finished for her granddaughter to wear somewhere that night. Sewing for herself, her children, her grandchildren, and her great-grandchildren was like the cobbler's shoes; her own clothes were often pinned together, and teaching her skills to others was never to her liking.

Mrs. Rucker was essentially modest; she never went out of her room without being fully clothed, including corsets. The worst whipping I ever got was for going to get a drink from the cooler in the lobby, the lobby full of men, and me with no panties under my dress.

Minnie was the girl from Headsville who never went to college, was well read, and knew the dictionary page by page. She had been able to answer her husband Henry's question: "Minnie, where is Eggwipt?" With laughter, the interpretation was "Egypt." The correction of "victiny" for "vicinity" was made of me — with a Master's degree from college.

Minnie's lifelong ambition was to be a nurse. She nursed her mother, her father, her children, her grandchildren. Sitting behind the counter, she wrote a letter to her niece, Vance: "I never have colds anymore. When I feel one coming on, I get a small bottle of camphor, wet the end of my finger in it, and apply to my nostrils, inhaling the vapor. Don't try to drop it in the nose as it is too strong. Then I touch my tongue to the bottle and let the saliva drop down my throat. This is the best and simplest thing for colds I have ever tried. Hope you will get some immediately and give it a try." How happy she was when her granddaughter, Frances, became a nurse!

It was Mama's nature to be hopeful and to look on the bright side of things. She wrote to another niece, "I am a lover of chickens. I have fifteen hens and nine little chicks now. They are Buff Opringtons and will multiply. I have a good garden spot; it was crowded out with weeds this year, but I have it nice and clean now, and hope to have a great garden next year." In addition to all her other duties, she was a canner of meat, home grown vegetables, and fruits like peaches and pears.

Mama's hotel was Mama's home. During the years, numerous relatives came to visit her. Mama always met them at the door, threw her arms around them, and they felt a happy sense of family. Her brother, Tom, for example, had died recently. His wife, Fanny, came and brought her three girls, Vada, Alma, and Iva. Minnie took the girls to a local hat shop and bought them each a red hat.

Her sister Maris Erwin arrived from Oklahoma. With her were her four children, including one named Sam. Minnie thought that not one of them must have ever had a decent meal in his life. They followed her around whining jealously, ''I wanna piece. Sam's gotta piece.'' It was the grandson of Maris who became Oral Roberts of later television fame.

The only one of Minnie's immediate family living in Franklin was her sister Nan. Nan's girls, Eula, Nannie, and Lottie, were very close to their Aunt Minnie; also her boys, Ernest, Bruce, and Jim. And Alys — well, she was something special, always warm, full of life—enough like her Aunt Minnie to really be her own daughter. She had many visits with her sister Sally's children and brother Pete's.

Through the years, however, Minnie spoke often of her brother Nat—the nearest of her brothers and sisters in age and in love. She remembered the December night when he had returned home after having to swim a nearby river. He had taken off his overcoat and it had stood on the floor, alone, frozen. Minnie often told of the many parallels in their lives— their marriages, the births of their first children. No, life would never be the same without Nat. She remembered what he had written so long ago in her autograph book:

> ''Should fortune smile on Thee
> and pleasant make thy lot,
> Dear sister, think of me
> and pray, forget me not.
> Should fortune frown on thee,
> and trouble gather fast.
> You have a friend where
> friendship long shall last.''

Minnie liked to reminisce. She often told stories she had heard about the Holtons coming to Texas from Macon, Georgia in a covered wagon driven by oxen. Her parents had stopped for two weeks in Jasper, Texas waiting for her, Minnie, to be born. "Ruthie", she said, "I want to tell you about when my parents moved on to dear old Robertson County. My brother, Billy, stayed in Jasper; there to marry, there to raise his family. Jasper seemed as far away then as New York is today."

Mama remembered she had worked hard in her father's house to pay for the marker for her first husband's — Jim's — grave. The Woodmen of the World later bought a marker for her second husband's — Henry's — grave. Mama said, "I want them both to lie together so I can grieve for both of them in that homey cemetery at Headsville by the side of dear old Ebenezer Church." Many years later, her children were to lay her remains in the peaceful cemetery. Some day my own daughter, Jean, will lay her mother to rest beside my mother.

Then Mama's mind wandered to tales which she had told me so often of old John, harnassed to the family surrey or the wagon, going unerringly to the same shady spot in front of old Ebenezer Church where he would stand — unhitched — for hours. "I tell you, Ruthie, I remember vividly the day my mother's foot missed the bottom step of the surrey, resulting in her broken hip. I can still feel the same numbness that I felt that morning I went into the house and unpacked my clothes — all ready to go to Baylor Female College in Belton. I realized that someone had to cook and wash, and iron for my father and the boys; and my mother could no longer do it." The next year, Jim Weeden had come along; she had loved him; she married him; she buried him; she had borne his daughter. She was only fifteen, a wife instead of a girl, ripe for the experiences college had to offer.

Mama always loved to take pictures. Many of the events of her life were preserved in the pictures which she placed in a rounded-corner album. She had only a tintype of Jim Weeden, but she prized it highly; it and her daughter Jimmie were all that she had to remind her of that gay young Lothario who had

15

passed through her life so long ago. One of her favorite pictures was of my father, Henry, herself, and my brother Robert and sister Jimmie as small children. They were all sitting on the front porch of their little two-room house at Bald Prairie. Mama was seated, warm, motherly, and relaxed. Henry was seated by her side, serious, strict, and dependable. A hound lurked under the front steps.

Yet, now I can look at this same picture which hangs on the wall of my apartment and I see that Mama, too, had those characterisitics. She had the ability to adapt herself to every mishap of life, to gather up the loose ends and go forward. Her backbone was straight. Nothing deterred her. Mama gave to all of us whatever abilities we have to stand up to life's vicissitudes. She was as sturdy as an oak.

At times, then, I was bored by Mama's oft-repeated stories of her early life. Now, I wish that I had listened more carefully. They are a great part of my heritage. Too bad that we have to grow "too soon old and too late wise." How I wish that I was able to set down more of Mama's recollections; that would be worthwhile. But now, I guess I'd better get back to the things I do remember about our life in the National Hotel.

We had only one picture show a week in Franklin. On Friday and Saturday nights, our family usually took off—en masse! Few drummers came to a small town over the weekend anyway, and Mr. Silverman was always around in case anyone did come. Everything was left wide open at the hotel. A note, posted on the front door, listed vacant rooms and stated: "Gone to the picture show. Be back by 7:30." Mama took her little purse in her hands; we crossed by a dirt road; and we were off to that magic place where "visions of sugar plums floated in our heads." We were to be entertained by the antics of Charlie Chaplin; we were to be enamored of Rudolph Valentino; we were to be thrilled, week after week, by the exploits of Pearl White. Yeah, those were the days!

Sometimes, my sister Jimmie played the piano at the picture show. This was before movies had sound tracks, so they were completely silent. She described her job there: "I figured

16

out music which fitted the scene and played it to get the audience in the mood. The most popular song I played was *Whispering,* a suitable song for love scenes; but when I'd play *Home on the Range* in western movies, the people in the audience would stomp and gallop with the deer and the antelope.''

On the day Jimmie got married, Mama summed up her life. ''I am a Hotel owner and manager. Twice widowed from fine young men. My daughter, Jimmie Weeden Garrett, gone on the train off to the home of her husband, Frank, in faraway West Virginia. Oh, what a send-off my family and Franklin friends had given them at the railroad station across the street. But that is all over, and I am back at the National Hotel — alone, except for Ruth.''

She rushed in to prepare supper for Mr. Silverman and the other guests. Gradually she became conscious that I, her youngest, was nowhere to be found. After searching all of my favorite haunts, Mama discovered me sitting dejectedly all alone in the middle of the front porch steps. I looked up at her and sobbed, ''Mama, I hate men. I hate the man you called my father. Sometimes I hate my brother. I hate Frank Garrett. Oh, Mama, I never intend to marry — as long as I can help it.''

JIMMIE

II

"Heard melodies are sweet, but those unheard are sweeter."

— *John Keats*

With Emphasis on Jimmie Weeden Garrett Smith Called Jimmie, Mrs. Jimmie Smith, or Miss Jim.

Music was her life. Even with all her different experiences, the genuine reality was music. After looking over her entire life, I realize this, anew. It was her favorite theme in all existence: the sound of music!

As a child, Jimmie took no piano lessons. Her first playing had been done at old Ebenezer Church at Headsville. When her family went to church Old John always pulled their wagon. He seemed to enjoy hearing the piano playing and the congregation singing. When they sang *The Church in the Wildwood,* that horse honestly looked all around as if he was as happy as they were when they sang *Amazing Grace.*

At singing conventions sister played the organ but her legs were too short to reach the pedals, so Grandpa Holton, the first president of the Robertson County Singing Convention, pumped the pedals, while Jimmie sat on his lap and played the songs. Invariably she played with no notes — just playing by ear, the surest proof of her love for music.

Jimmie worked hard when she went to Baylor College. Her statement was: "I practice long hours on music which I never even had a chance to hear before." When she applied for work at the telephone office in Franklin, she asked, "May I take night duty, so I can teach music lessons in the day?" As she taught a boy later,

> "Poems are made by fools like me,
> But only God can make a tree."

So she considered music; only God could make beautiful music.

Jim Weeden, her father, was not a settler. He wanted to head West, had a roaming look in his eyes. When he first arrived at Grandpa Holton's house in the country, he was riding on a horse and playing a guitar. This made him ideal for Jimmie's father.

There was more than one echo of her father in the child—Jimmie. Her eyes were jumping. Minnie, her mother-to-be, had been left alone with the sick Jim Weeden while her father, Thomas Holton, went to Kosse for a doctor. Before he left, Minnie inquired frantically, "You're not going to leave us here all alone?"

To which her father replied: "Yes, I have to. Are you afraid?"

Her eyes searched the surrounding darkness; she thought she heard a rustling in a nearby bush. Then she saw Jim's beloved pale face in the flickering light from the table lamp and answered with a contempt for danger: "No, papa, I'm not afraid."

After her father's departure, Minnie had sat there by the bed, cradling Jim's head—her own body jumping convulsively in rhythm to Jim's eyes which were going back and forth, back and forth, in his head, as if in consternation at his early tragic death. At last Minnie fell asleep. Just fifteen years old and waiting for Jimmie to be born — with eyes that jumped — though in her case the movement was more like a twinkle. If one can believe an old wives' tale, Jimmie was marked with the movement of her father's eyes and her mother's body.

A few years later, Minnie had married Henry Rucker, a school teacher in the community, and they soon went to live in Franklin. As a young girl, Jimmie had the usual experiences of a small town person. Once she went with others on a picnic to Indian Mound—east of town—where they went for arrowheads. When she was older, she went on a possum hunt on a moonlight night—well chaperoned of course. An old Mexican man, wearing a colorful sombrero and pushing a cart containing an old lard can up and down the streets, was seen frequently in Franklin. He shouted his wares with the cadence of a song:

> "Hot Tamales!
> Hot Tamales!
> Buy your Hot Tamales!
> Very Hot; Very Good!
> Home made Hot Tamales!
> Four bits a dozen!"

These three experiences gave rise to lifelong interests. Jimmie always loved the out of doors though she never had much time to enjoy it. Years later she lived with Mama at the old Hurley house in Franklin. There she kept the grass and flowers — a show case for all the town to see. In Dallas, she would often take long walks with Frances; the well cared for flower beds were a delight, and the songs of the birds echoed in her own musician's ears. Often when they went home they ate Mexican food — Jimmie's favorite — particularly Wolf Brand Chili.

Frequently, she went to all-day dinner and singing on the ground, at least that's the way they put it in Franklin. There she could play and sing — indulging in her favorite form of entertainment.

The main street of Franklin was covered with huge shade trees; on this street Uncle Sid Ferguson was frequently seen. He was an old man that had the first phonograph Jimmie ever saw. Much later she was to hear soul searching music played by master hands on modern phonographs, on radio, and even the television; but nothing compared with the music of that first phonograph. Some boys and girls would go up to Uncle Sid's house to play it. They were enamoured with the big horn, shaped like a morning glory blossom. The records were cylinder shaped — not like today's platter records. What a break it was for a girl whose whole life was to be devoted to music!

Jimmie went with Kitty Davlin, one of her best friends, to dances, skating rinks, parties, joy rides — all sorts of places. And once, Mama took Kitty to Galveston with Jimmie, Ruth, and Alys Truett; how funny their bathing suits looked in pictures taken then but looked at long after! Jimmie's sparkling blue eyes, her dazzling complexion, and her strawberry colored hair made her an asset to any group.

The girls went down to the tournament troop trains later on and took the boys going through coffee, cookies, and sandwiches. They stood there by the trains and sang with the boys such old songs as "By the Light of the Silvery Moon" and "I'm Gonna Call You My Sweetheart." There were so many occasions that Mama wanted Sister to keep a diary or a scrapbook of remembrances. Sister often thought about it, but her life was crammed so full that she never seemed to get around to it.

When Jimmie was eighteen, she went away to college — Normal School at Huntsville for one year. This was the custom for training teachers in that day. During the Christmas holidays, I was born — a real top crop for my family. Jimmie loved her little sister, Ruth, very dearly and considered me her special charge. In return, I adored her and I have always considered myself lucky to have had a big sister.

That summer, the tragic events related in Chapter III took place, and Jimmie went with Mama to live at the National Hotel. Life in the hotel just seemed to be made for my sister, now known to everyone as "Miss Jim." During the year she taught in rural schools near Franklin. These were happy times for her.

Then Frank Garrett came along. He was an itinerant photographer who stayed at the hotel and went out to surrounding towns to drum up business. His family lived in West Virginia — far away. Quite a different sort of life from Jimmie's in Texas. He fell in love with my beautiful sister with her strawberry hair and dancing blue eyes, and soon they were married. They lived for a while at the National Hotel.

Alys Truett, our cousin, had always been a very good friend to Jimmie. Once, when they were little girls living at Headsville, they had gone out to the four-holer privy behind the house. Jimmie told Alys about some freshly dug earth to the side of the privy. The girls took a nearby shovel and dug into the earth. They found a metal box buried there containing much money—

all in silver. Tash (as everyone called Alys) was shocked, but Jimmie, who always seemed to have a good solution, reassured her: "That's not so strange, Tash. Very few people in the Baptist Church have paper money."

But Alys, still not understanding, said, "But—but—how on earth did this get here?"

Jimmie answered. "I'll bet I know. Uncle Polk is church treasurer. Your daddy must have hidden the money here till he had time to go to Kosse and put it in the bank." The girls kept this secret forever. No one knew then nor till nearly one hundred years later about Uncle Polk's metal box containing the church money.

It was customary for Alys to spend many nights with Jimmie, particularly after they were grown. She continued this practice even after Sister was married. One night Alys spent the night sleeping in an adjoining room to Jimmie's and Frank's — upstairs. In the middle of the night she was awakened by most unusual sounds; the next morning she talked to Jimmie about them.

"Hey, Jim, last night I heard the queerest sounds. I can't imagine what was going on."

Jimmie was embarrased. "Oh, Tash! You always put your foot in it when you get started."

"Well, I only wanted to know what was happening."

Jimmie answered: "If you must know (red faced but teasing) Frank and I were just pitching a little woo."

Alys replied: "These damned walls are so all-fired thin. Well, I guess I've got a pretty good idea of how to act when I get married."

The couple lived in Franklin for awhile, and her brother Robert played a big part in their lives. The boys figured a livery stable business would really pay off. A great many people didn't have any way to get to places, and Frank thought they'd come in and rent the equipment. They convinced Mama that a lot of drummers at the hotel would like to go out to other towns to sell their products. So she came through, as usual, and financed their business. One of the best features was that Jimmie could go to social affairs in a "hug-me-tight" buggy. But money was scarce, and soon Frank became dissatisfied. They lost the money they had put into the venture; neither man considered Mama, who had put up the money in the first place.

Then they moved to Winters in West Texas. Frank had heard a hotel drummer at the hotel say one day: "I know of a damned good business in a town in West Texas — Winters."

Frank, all agog, asked, "Does it take much capital?"

"No, not much."

After investigation, Brother Frank had decided to go. Robert (via Mama) went into the cleaning and pressing business with him. Sister would say to the two men on Sunday morning, "Why don't you both go with me to Sunday School and Church today?"

Frank answered. "Afraid we can't go this morning. We have to clean up our place nice for next week's trade."

Robert just put in a weak, "Naw, Sis, haf to do this, you know."

So Jimmie, sadly, went on to church without them. Soon her sadness turned to gladness because she was always happiest when she was playing and singing in church. But the town was not very prosperous. They lost money again, of course—Mama's again, certainly. Soon the couple went to West Virginia to live with Frank's parents, and Robert came back to Franklin.

That next year, 1912, proved very long for all of us. West Virginia (as I found out in our atlas) was so far away with Constance born there and all. Finally, Sister wrote that she was pregnant again. This decided Mama. Nothing daunted, she planned and executed a trip to West Virginia, via New Orleans and New York, taking Alys Truett and me (just 7 years old) with her. The hotel was left for two months in the capable hands of Mrs. Scott, who later became Alys' mother-in-law.

The voyage from New Orleans to New York was wonderful, but I became quite ill there and had to stay in the hotel with a hired nursemaid (as baby-sitters were called then.) On Sunday morning, Mama and Tash sailed forth in search of a Baptist church; then they took in the Statue of Liberty and all the famous New York sights in true Texas style. But the best part of the trip was arriving in the beautiful country of West Virginia and seeing my very own niece, Constance, soon to be shortened to Connie. She was so adorable, and I fell for her at sight.

We loved all of Brother Frank's family and enjoyed the horseback rides and picnics. At Mama's insistence, we even went down to see a mine in operation. But the time was fast approaching for our departure for home. Mama begged for Sister and the baby to go back to Texas with her—wishing for her second child to be born in her mother's home state and using the argument that she (Mama) wanted to share in Jimmie's care. She promised that she would send them all three back to West Virginia on the train just as soon as the new baby was able to travel.

Sister had been rather quiet during our entire visit. She seemed withdrawn and unhappy—not at all her usual jolly self. Brother Frank was seldom at home. He always came up with a mumbled, lame excuse about "seeing some friends." Mama found him willing for Sister and Connie to go back with us, and Mother Garrett thought the trip would do Jimmie good. So it was decided that they were to go. On the train, Sister told Mama about the rift with Frank. Distance did not seem to make Brother Frank's heart grow fonder, and the upshot was that Jimmie and her two babies came to live at the hotel in Franklin with us. I loved having them, the two children particularly; and I considered Frances my special property since she was born at our hotel.

One day in December, Jimmie received a letter from Frank. It was in response to one she had written to him. She opened it and read it. "Mama," she called, "I'd like for you to see this."

Mama took the letter and read: "Dear Jimmie, you say you and the children need winter clothes. Here is some money. I don't remember the winters there being very cold. Besides, I have some heavy expenses just now. Maybe I can send more in a few months. Frank."

"And this is what he sent," said Jimmie tearfully. "A five dollar bill! And he never said a word about my offer to come back to West Virginia to try again." Sister considered the five dollar bill for winter clothes for the three of them an insult, so she returned it.

This was the last letter she was ever to receive from him. He never even saw Frances. Three years later he received an uncontested divorce, and Sister began to make a new life in Franklin, Texas.

Soon after, Robert's first wife, Ruth, died, and he brought his two children, Robert and Minnie, home to Mama. So her four grandchildren grew up in Mammy's (as she was lovingly termed) hotel together. The four children seemed like Minnie's own children; and the life of a small town hotel was the only life they ever knew. I never realized any differences in the children. In fact, I ran home from school one day crying inconsolably because someone had told me that Jimmie was my half sister. I loved the "kids" equally. They were my charges, my responsibilities, my joy!

During the next several years, Mama left the hotel occasionally; but she always returned. Minnie was known for her wandering foot but the hotel — all paid for — was her security. First, she left for Gainesville, to run a hotel there. Second, she went to Waco to be near Robert with his children before he was sent overseas in World War I from Richfield Air Force Base; but he spent the whole war near Waco. Third, Mama moved to Austin so that I would transfer to Texas University, but my ties to Baylor College were too strong and I stayed in Belton. Mama ran a rooming house and sold hats and corsets. Oh, yes, I forgot one other escape from the hotel. She built a house in Franklin and moved the family there. I remember that all the kids had measles and mumps at this house, but I cared for them and never did take either. Sometimes when Mama went on these escapades she rented the hotel to Mrs. Scott or Mrs. Talley, but usually it was to Jimmie. She knew the hotel business as well as Mama did. Her friendliness and good humor made the guests feel very welcome; so Jimmie was a real replacement for Mama — even in the way she picked up a bit of crochet — never letting her hands be idle. Who could foretell that years later the pieces were to be crocheted together to make a bedspread for each granddaughter.

Sister gave this account of her life in Franklin while she was raising her children: "I could always find employment because I was loyal and willing to work, so we didn't have to want for money. There was always a job for me with the telephone office, and the girls at any time could work at the hotel. Sometimes they would need me to spend the night to work at the telephone office. Oh, the late calls! You'd be surprised at the people who were called at all hours; but — No! No! I can't tell you a thing about them. A telephone has no ears. I was Worthy Matron of the Eastern Star for two years; thank goodness I'm just a member now. Of course I keep busy as church pianist — what with practicing for special numbers and all.

"I'll tell you what really makes life in Franklin worthwhile though—friendship! My friends in Franklin came from all walks of life, but the ones I love the most and who return my affection are the other girls who work at the telephone office."

Mr. Silverman was a guest at the hotel all the time sister lived there. She would say to him: "Mr. Abe, look after my children this afternoon, please; don't let them play out in the street."

And he answered: "Sure. And I'm proud to be a help to you, Miss Jim. Here, scalawags, Connie, Frances, Minnie, Robert; I've got a quarter. Let's go up the street and have an ice cream cone." Sister would invite him to go to church on Sunday mornings. One day he told her, "Miss Jim, I do not believe in God. I think a man is like a dog; when he dies, he dies all over." But Mr. Silverman's heart was in the right place and he was always ready to help others, particularly children; as witness the sidewalk which he had placed all around the new school building.

One of the most interesting men in Franklin was Mr. George C. Parnum. He spoke often of his former life: "I have a wife and family in London. By Jove, I left England many years ago, but I'm still remembered there." (No one knew the cause of his departure, but years after his death, a son came to

Franklin and put a marker on his grave.) The old man would drive up and down the street with his horses, Sweetheart and Darling, pulling his old fashioned 'Surrey with the fringe on top.' In his musical voice, he'd call out:

"Come on, boys and girls,
I'll take you for a ride
With my Sweetheart and my Darling
And we will on a picnic go
Be very careful, though,
Of red bugs, ticks and mosquitoes."

Mr. Parnum had been a music publisher in London; now he sold music to his fellow townspeople in his adopted country. He also tuned pianos, collected junk, and even taught a few private piano pupils. In his old ragged clothes he would go to the Baptist Church on Sunday and play the violin. When he played, it seemed as if the gates of heaven opened up and one could imagine that the angels were playing on their harps. Just as when Uncle Polk Truett lifted up his head to pray; then one could imagine that the very voice of God was talking to him.

When my brother Robert was living on the old Holomon Ranch, he went fox hunting often. He told of one of his experiences. "I was walking along and heard a faint sound in the distance. I listened intently, and as I got closer I could tell it was someone playing a fiddle. When I got near enough to see, I recognized Old Man Parnum playing his violin, playing Beethoven with an audience of birds and bees, and occasionally (as now) a dog and a man. I observed that the old man was actually living in an empty piano box. Sleeping, eating, surviving in that one small piano box — yet creating beautiful music."

Jimmie also told of an experience with Mr. Parnum. "One day I took my daughters with me to buy some music from him in his little old delapidated house in Franklin. When we got inside, I detected the presence of music everywhere. Tables were covered with sheets of beautiful songs; stacks were on all the chairs; dresser drawers were stuffed to overflowing with instrumental selections; they were scattered all over the cook stove and the bed. Mr. Parnum literally *slept* on music . . . and I had a feeling of kinship with the lonely old man.''

Often, in the evening, a group of people would gather around the piano in Mama's parlor — that parlor with the white wicker furniture, the old phonograph with the picture of the listening dog, with family portraits all around, and with books everywhere, overflowing the hand made bookcases. They were gathering to sing after supper for recreation. (There was no radio or television in the early nineteenth century, and there were few automobiles for joy rides.) An occasional drummer joined the group. Mr. Firm Carpenter, the local postmaster, and his wife usually sang with them. So did Tom Hawkins, Alys Truett, Mr. Sam Rogers and Miss Maud McMillan — the couple that never married but courted for years. Mr. Will Rushing was also with the singers. He was a tall, handsome old bachelor — as typical a lawman as Marshall Dillon on television in the far distant future.

Jimmie led the group. She loved to play the piano; and they wanted to hear her play the old songs like *Whispering, Who's Sorry Now?* and *Let the Rest of the World Go By.*

Sometimes the four children and I were allowed to join the group. Connie and Frances would slip in close under the piano when their mother played their favorites, *Napoleon's Last Charge* and *Maple Leaf Rag.* Connie played them when she grew up; later her daughter, JoAn, played them too. Then her granddaughter, Connie Marie, also learned to play them — making the love of music go on from generation to generation.

During World War I the group sang war songs: ''Over There'', ''How You Gonna Keep 'Em Down On The Farm'', and ''It's A Long Way To Tipperary'', ''Goodbye Broadway, Hello France'', and ''Just A Baby's Prayer At Twilight''. I still remember every word of them.

On November 11, 1918, Germany surrendered to the Allies. The word was received in Franklin very early in the morning. Morgan had just come to the Hotel to cook breakfast when all the whistles began blowing, the church bells started pealing, and all the people were aroused to scream and yell at the top of their voices.

Morgan gave us all a dishpan and a long spoon to beat in celebration. Mama, Sister, the four children and I were enthusiastic participants in this parade. I remember that I had been secretly jealous of Mama's marching at the head of a group of women shouting for "Susan B. Anthony" and "the Women's Christian Temperance Union." Now I was a real part of a real parade.

So life went on full of happiness and sadness, frustration and fulfillment until Jimmie married Mr. Smith, an old beau from Sam Houston State College. He met her on a train on the way to Huntsville; at school he dated her and wanted to marry; but they never did, and he found himself in Sanderson, where he was principal of the high school many years later, holding a conversation with a fellow teacher.

"I didn't know that you lived in Franklin. The sweetest gal I ever knew lived there."

"Really? What was her name?"

"Jimmie Weeden. Her mother was Mrs. Minnie Rucker. She ran a hotel there."

"Why, you can't mean it. I know Mrs. Rucker well. By the way, Mama wrote me the other day that Mrs. Rucker's daughter, Jimmie, had come home from West Virginia to live in Franklin with her two little girls."

"I can't believe it," Mr. Smith said interestedly. "I wonder what happened to Frank."

"Why don't you write her a letter and find out."

So on this challenge, Archie Smith wrote to Jimmie Garrett that night. Their friendship developed through letters; he wrote her that he had always loved her; she needed a home and father for her daughters; the result was that he came to Franklin and married her Christmas Eve, 1918. Connie was six and Frances was five. Neither remembered her own father.

They lived the first few months in Sanderson. Jimmie and the girls missed Mama and the Hotel very much. A. W. was trying to find some other way to make a living besides teaching. Frances prattled: "The big oil wells look like big old trees reaching out with their arms to get us."

When they moved to Breckenridge, they rode on a train pass. That was a big thrill for the girls who clamored for an ice cream cone like Mr. Silverman's, which they were given for a special treat. Strange! But not even Baskin-Robbin's tastes as good. While they were there, Sister left the children one day for a few hours with "Daddy Smith". In their play, they breathed their breath against a window pane to see it get cloudy. Mr. Smith was quite indignant and started to whip them but remembered — in time — Sister's oft-repeated admonitions against his temper. It was one of their chief bones of contention.

But the place that seemed most like home was near Marshall in East Texas where A.W. had spent his childhood. One of their chief delights was riding on Old Dexter, their gentle retired dray horse. Frances, who was always into some kind of mischief, took a freshly baked loaf of bread from the kitchen. Connie wanted to go too, so they both climbed on Old Dexter's back and rode him down the hill.

The lazy sights and sounds of a spring morning tempted them and they went much farther then just "down the hill", eating all the while on the insides of the loaf of bread. When they reached down to get Old Dexter, he gave a big lunge and away he went back home to his shady pasture. Both girls fell off and had to walk all the way back home. They had considerable difficulty in explaining away the middle of the loaf of bread which Frances still clutched in her grubby little hand. You can bet that they were punished when their mother came home that same afternoon. Their stepfather had been forbidden ever to lay a hand on them; Sister ruled the roost with a firm hand.

Jimmie attended the College of Marshall part-time and worked as a bookkeeper part-time at the co-op store to supplement their lean income. Finally, however, A.W. had to go back to teaching, and he found a job at Spicewood — near Austin.

They decided that Jimmie should go to Baylor College, where Ruth was, to pursue her degree in voice. Archie said: "I am very anxious for you to go. Next year I will be making $125.00 per month. I can live on $50.00 and you can go to school on the other $75.00. Mama, always ready for anyone to pursue an education, wanted to keep the two children. "Why I'll hardly know they are on the place. They can play with Minnie and Robert, and they'll be a real help to me in the Hotel; I won't even miss what they'll eat." So this was the arrangement for a year.

The second year, Jimmie was allowed to teach younger students at the college, so she took the children to live with her in an apartment in Belton. These were extremely happy years for Jimmie. Beethoven, Mendelssohn, Bach—many great names in music became actualities for her. Their wonderful sounds echoed in her head forever. Their music seemed to give her a sense of permanence, a feeling that life was good.

.   Then, they moved to Wheelock, where Mr. Smith had a better job, as superintendent. The whole family was really content in Wheelock. It was an old, aristocratic town, which Jimmie found to be very receptive to music. She gave many excellent recitals, both individually and with her students. Connie still says: "We never lived anywhere that we had better, more congenial friends. And we were so nice and close to Franklin and could frequently visit Mammy, Aunt Ruth, (who was teaching there at the time), Robert and Minnie at the National Hotel—which we always considered home."

At school one day, a teacher told Frances to stay in after school for some infraction of the rules. Just as school closed, Mrs. Smith came by—not realizing what the teacher had told Frances—and ordered: "Frances, go home quickly now. Don't dawdle. Connie has to practice, and I'll be home in about an hour." Frances went straight home, listening to her mother's command; she didn't understand all the rules in Wheelock anyway.

Soon after Connie and Sister got home, Mr. Smith came stalking in talking distractedly: "Frances, come here. Since when do you think the superintendent's child is more important than any other child and does not have to obey the teacher. I'm going to whip you for sure this time." But Sister intervened:

32

"A.W., I didn't know that Frances had been told to stay in. I told her to come on home. The child is not to blame. If anyone is at fault, it is her mother." Well, Mr. Smith didn't want to whip them both, so he went for about an hour's walk, but Frances shook for the entire hour.

The last place they lived together was Franklin. Mr. Smith was teaching in Buffalo. Connie was a grown girl then and soon married Sylman Galloway. Mr. Smith was outspoken in his criticisms of them and of Jimmie. So she decided they would be better off without him; and in 1930, they were separated and later divorced.

The hardest period of sister's life occurred at the time that should have been the most peaceful. The depression hit hard and it was almost impossible to make ends meet. Her oldest daughter was married to a boy that did not have sufficient training to make a good living for his family. Her youngest daughter was at Providence Hospital in Waco learning to be a nurse and not yet able to make a living.

Sister expressed it this way: "I work long hours at my telephone job and then teach as many music students as I possibly can. I buy things on credit. I borrow money. Mama can't help much because the hotel business isn't as good as it used to be. She often sends me very welcome left-over food from the meals served at the National Hotel, but I get in deeper all the time. Yet I always go to church whenever I can; it is my pleasure to sing and play for others. Music has always been first with me, except for my children and grandchildren."

JoAn, Connie and Sylman's first child, was loved by everyone. She was the darling of four families — her own, her two grandmother's and her great-grandmother's.

They moved to a little house near the telephone office where there was room for the children in about 1931. Sylvia Nan was born there; Frances had come home to help because she was an obstetric nurse. Connie was having an exceedingly hard time and her mother had to leave the room. She turned toward the parlor distractedly mumbling the words: "When hope is gone, one has to depend on God." Then she reached upward with

33

both hands on the paper covered wall as if God indeed were there and she could reach Him. Sylvia's first wail filled the air, and Jimmie knew that all was well. Orrel Jean soon joined the family. They were the dearest three little sisters imaginable. Robert Frost said, "All I know about life is: It goes on." Even so did Sister's.

After both her children had left, Sister lived by the water tower — all alone. For many years she had been the mainstay of her family — breadwinner, guide and consultant. Connie's troubles had been her own. Frances' training had been her care. When these responsibilities were no longer on her shoulders, she had a nervous breakdown. After awhile, she went to Skidmore where Connie and Sylman and their children lived.

Jimmie wrote this in a letter to her mother: "I am very happy here in Skidmore with Connie and her family. Her dear children are like my very own — not only JoAn and Sylvia Nan and Orrel Jean, but also Robert Sylman who came later. I love them all dearly. Sylman is just like my own son and Connie and I have never been closer, even in the good old days when we planned for her to be a concert pianist. That's one of the most wonderful things about music. It enriches life; and regardless of whether one plays on the stage or in her own little cottage, life is more worthwhile."

When the time came for her return to Franklin, she did so with renewed strength, able to take up her life again — to go on.

When Mama retired from the hotel, she went to Tyler to live with me where I was teaching. But I left to become service club hostess in the Army, and later married and went to live in California. Mama lived in an apartment at Alys' and then bought the old Hurley place in Franklin, and she and Sister lived there until Mama's death on May 13, 1952.

After several years, filled with many more responsibilities, Sister became physically ill and went to live with Frances and Doyle in Dallas. Despite her pain and suffering, she was always happy with them. Frances devoted herself to making her mother's last years as comfortable and happy as she could. She took her mother across the city to take private lessons in playing

34

the pipe organ — one of Jimmie's lifelong ambitions. Her occasional visits to Connie were happy times; but Sister developed Parkinson's Disease. Later she broke a hip, so her children had to have additional help, and they placed her in a nursing home. She was in several homes in Dallas, then in South Texas. Both Connie and Frances took excellent care of her. Frances went every day to feed her mother and bathe and dress her and push her in her wheelchair up and down the halls.

In the nursing home for the first few years, she frequently played and sang in the parlors. One day they were listening to Perry Como singing "Ave Maria." Frances says that she can still hear her mother say, "I'll just tell you he can sure sing a lot better than that Presley boy." Sister loved this happy time. She felt that life was made better for the other people who were there. What more can music do?

But the time soon came when even her love for music was no longer in evidence. Her days were spent in her own room except for little rides in the wheelchair. Sister's lovely appearance, her beautiful hair, and her disregard for her own feelings gave others cheer. Old songs echoed in her brain and brought a little smile to the corners of her mouth.

She might well have ended her life with the words of a song which she had once sung so beautifully:

"I sing because I'm Happy;
I sing because I'm Free.
For His eye is on the Sparrow,
And I know He watches me."

BOB

III

"I am the Master of my fate."

— *William Ernest Henly*

With Emphasis on Robert Lee Rucker Called Bob.

Bang! The sound of the shotgun shattered the lazy hum of the quietude of a sunny morning on a Texas farm. A startled expression rushed to the face of the half-witted victim. A few seconds before, he had been brandishing the open straight-edged razor in his hand and shouting: "I'm gonng git ya, Bob. You had no business kickin' my pore defenseless dogs, you son of a b----." "At that inexorable moment the sound of the gun occurred simultaneously with the epithet and Miley Griswold staggered backward and fell off the porch into the plowed furrow of the cornfield — dead!

My brother, Robert, threw the door open and gazed, distractedly, for a moment. Instantly, he was on his knees, in consternation, cradling his friend's head in his arms. "Oh, Miley, I didn't mean to shoot you. I don't know how this rifle got in my hands. It was leaning against the wall behind the door. Miley it must have gone off when I slammed the door to keep you and your razor outside. I warned you not to let them damned pigs get out and into my corn crop again, but I didn't mean to shoot you. Oh, Miley, I've killed you."

Robert's mind recoiled from the memory of that other tragedy which had happened only ten short years before—when he was just a boy of 14. He heard again, the voice of his father, Henry Rucker, repeatedly resounding in his ears: "No son of mine could be dumb enough to fail Latin a second time. I'm gonna give you a real licking this time." The crumpled report card had fallen, forgotten, to the floor.

Robert felt once more the impact of the buggy whip against his shoulders, the buggy whip that was supposed to lean against the wall behind the door. He sensed rather than saw his mother fall into the waiting chair as she was thrust aside. Again his father's voice boomed: "No, you don't, Minnie. You'll not protect your worthless son this time."

In a flash of memory he could see his Grandfather Holton stumbling in at the front door with his open pocketknife in his right hand—that right arm had been stiff since he was wounded at Appomattox fighting the Yankees. The old man had been whittling out on the front steps, as was his habit. He mumbled from the doorway, "What's going on in here?" His stiff right arm was extended in front of him, his whittling knife still gripped in the fingers of his hand. "Why, what's the matter, Minnie?" At the sound from the doorway, his son-in-law, Henry Rucker, had wheeled around and into the knife held in the old man's hand, plunging it deep into his own abdomen. Henry fell, fatally stabbed, to the floor.

Instantly, Grandpa Holton was on his knees cradling his son-in-law's head in his arms. "Oh, Henry, you done it to yourself. You knowed my arm was stiff. Oh, Henry, I've killed you. I didn't mean to do it." But in two months, he was dead from gangrene, and the office of County Clerk of Robertson County was vacant.

The sound of their voices reverberated down the ringing corridors of time. Their incessant pealing forever blotting out Robert's counter desires, his better impulses, his futile attempts at stifling their damning intonation. There remained only a helpless, hopeless feeling. Nothing that Mama could say or do; no help that she could give him ever sufficed to overcome this fanatical impression. Never to realize his own potential! Never to have true, lasting happiness! Never to accomplish those things of which he was capable! Brother never attended school again. The victim of circumstance and heredity. Forever cursed by the visitation of his father and his grandfather before him.

I was only a tiny girl, but I felt the real anguish of my older brother, Robert. It was this tragic accident which brought a young lawyer, Pat Neff, from Waco down to Franklin. He was the counsel for the prosecution in the trial of Robert Lee Rucker for murder. Mama employed local lawyers Mr. Grady Goodman and Mr. Henry Bush to defend her son.

For two weeks the trial went on there in the county court-house of Robertson County. That trial in which all the dirty linens of previous Ruckers and Holtons had been aired. That trial in which the local lawyers had so doggedly defended Robert Rucker. That trial in which my brother had been finally acquitted of murder.

Every day young Mr. Neff had eaten at my mother's table at the National Hotel. Every night he had slept as a paying guest in her house. One day—near the end of his stay—the following conversation had ensued.

"Mrs. Rucker, will you please be so kind as to figure my bill. My plans are to depart tomorrow after lunch."

"Yes, Mr. Neff; it will be ready for you," she said smilingly.

"May I be permitted to say, my dear Mrs. Rucker, that you look particularly happy today."

Minnie drew herself up to her full five feet five inches. "I am, thank you, Mr. Neff. My son has just been declared innocent. He is now a free man."

Mr. Neff stammered incoherently. "Your — your — son! Why, I had no idea! You must be — be — I had never — even — even connected the names. It is beyond my comprehension how you could have accorded me such excellent treatment and uncommon courtesy. Me, the attorney for the prosecution of your son."

"Why, sir. You were a guest in my hotel and in my home, and you deserved the same treatment as any other guest."

"May I say, Madam, that your son is a fine young man. I'm sure the jury made the right decision according to the law and the evidence. Man, in his wisdom, has never been able to devise a better plan when dealing with the life and liberty of an individual than to try him before a jury of his peers."

"Thank you, sir," Mrs. Rucker replied, "and may I say that we have never had a nicer guest at the hotel."

"Those are kind words, my dear lady. May I add that your own behavior has been exemplary."

This experience was to lead to two others later. The first, when Pat Neff was running for governor of Texas. By that time, Mama was a leader in the community and quite a politician herself. She had led parades, marching up and down the streets favoring *Votes for Women* and *W.C.T.U.* During his race, she had campaigned widely for candidate Neff.

One day Mama received the following handwritten note from Mr. Neff:

"My dear Mrs. Rucker,

I want to thank you again for your excellent treatment while I was a guest in your hotel many years ago. I know what a busy life you lead. I appreciate it more than tongue can tell that you paused amidst your toils to fight my battles and help me win my election to the high office of governor. There is no one in the whole of the Lone Star State whose support I value more highly than yours. It is to me a blessing and a happy recollection that will linger with me until the end of life.

Most sincerely yours,
Pat M. Neff"

The latter encounter I remember vividly. I was working on my masters' degree in speech at Northwestern University near Chicago. I had written to Mr. Neff asking his permission to use him and his speeches as my subject for a model persuasive speaker. He received me graciously; allowed me an interview; and presented me with two volumes of his speeches — recalling, all the while, his previous meetings with my mother and my brother.

For several years after Mama went into the hotel business, Brother acted as porter — meeting all the trains, carrying the baggage and escorting the traveling men across the street to the National Hotel. He filled the shoes of bell boy, chambermaid, and head waiter — sometimes even cook when Morgan failed to turn up.

But he was not a very dependable worker. Mr. Will Cofield, a frequent visitor to the hotel, might have said to a group of drummers: "Fellows, I tell you, Mrs. Rucker can have some of the best wild game to eat that you've ever licked your choppers over." Then, early the next morning, Bob would take French leave and go hunting all day and all night with two or three cronies — whom Mama denounced as "the scum of the earth."

Nearly always, they bagged considerable game: dove, quail, duck, squirrel — sometimes even venison. Mama would, of course, forgive him such forays despite the fact that she fussed almost constantly about his hunting and fishing, gambling and drinking, and carousing with the town sots. Often he went fishing on the Navasota River, locally called "the Navasot." Mama didn't like the river nor what went on there, such as drinking rot gut liquor and moonshine whiskey!

Hotel life grew a little confining for Bob's fancy; besides, Mama kept too tight a rein for his gambling tastes; so in a few years he moved out on a farm and visited the hotel only occasionally — bringing Mama watermelons, beans, peas and tomatoes. In the fall he would bring in a small hog or pig to be slaughtered in our back yard. At those times, Mama canned and preserved watermelon rinds, peas, juices, and made the best hog's head cheese I've ever tasted, not to mention pure pork sausage, crackling bread, chitlins, and pickled pigs feet. Brother's contributions to the meals were always welcome.

How well do I remember Brother teaching me to drive old Studey more than sixty years ago. Mama, always one to try the new, had bought one of the first cars in Franklin — to accommodate her wandering foot and to cultivate a love for traveling in all of us. It was a seven passenger model, built by the Studebaker Auto Company of South Bend, Indiana, and it sold for $685.00. The advertisement stated that the car had free wheeling in all forward speeds with cushion power — whatever that meant. I loved the fact that it was an open touring car with canvas sides that snapped on, containing little isinglass windows for protection from rain and cold. But the features that intrigued me most were the two jump seats that folded into the floor, and the marvelous way old Studey responded to Brother's driving. Our whole family went on jaunts all over Texas and several adjoining states. Sometimes with Brother at the wheel; sometimes with Mama; and occasionally — in later years — even me!

One of the most momentous occasions in my brother's life was when he was run over by a wagon with a load of 100 bales of hay. The horses shied at a paper blowing in the road, causing the rope which was tied around the hay to break. This threw Brother out and the wagon ran over him. He became so ill that he could not be taken to the hospital; consequently Mama had Dr. Howard Dudgeon, a surgeon from Waco, to come to see him. Later, Dr. Dudgeon told about this in a medical journal.

"We set up for the operation under the most primitive conditions — on a dining table on the back porch of the farm house. My surgeon's tools had been sterilized in a wash pan and there were plenty of sheets to be torn up for bandages. The people were hanging out of trees to watch the proceedings. When I stuck the first knife into his abdomen, the corruption gushed high."

Brother recovered from this operation, but had to have about ten other operations throughout the remainder of his life for adhesions and other difficulties developing from the injury. He always had a weak stomach and suffered intensely with indigestion, but he seldom took any medicine for any ailments. His horror was becoming addicted to drugs. He told me once: "When I got run over by that wagon, poor old Mammy sat by me and begged me to take morphine, but I chose not to."

Brother's first wife was named Ruth. She was a pretty, intelligent girl with long, beautiful hair worn braided around her head. Ruth was patient and longsuffering, but occasionally she would put her foot down and say, "Robert," in no uncertain terms. But they had only five short years together and Ruth died, one of the first victims of the flu. Brother brought their two little children to the hotel and said, "Here, Mama. Please take them and raise them just like they were your own." And so Robert and Minnie came to grow up in our home and to be just the same as my little brother and sister.

Brother then went to work for Uncle Sam on his old, early DC6 flying jennies. He fought the battle of Richfield in Waco, Texas. After he was discharged, the remainder of his life was spent going off on junkets and working at first one odd job and then another. He always seemed to live in the most out of the way, inaccessible spots that could be found. He worked as a driller in the oil fields; he helped to build Possum Kingdom Dam in West Texas. Brother also worked in Mexia. On this job as well as on others, Bob felt that he couldn't live up to Mama's expectations of him; he never seemed able to make a living.

In the early years he had a livery stable and ran a service car in Franklin. In between jobs he would settle down on a rented farm in some remote part of Robertson County to farm and hunt and fish and to raise and train hunting dogs. Once when his Model T exploded and burned up; once to make the down payment on a secluded farm in Arkansas; and on other occasions too numerous to mention, Brother would borrow some money at the First National Bank in Franklin. Mama always went on his note. Also, whenever Brother got too sick to work anywhere, Mama would get on the train and go to him; she would arrange for doctors and hospitals. As often as not, Mama would meet the obligations on the notes and pay the hospital bills herself. Brother would always promise to repay these debts, but he somehow forgot.

As a token of his good intentions one time when Bob came home from the oil fields he gave Mama $1,000.00 and bought her a rocking chair. This much for years of loving care for two children. Oh, yes, I forgot that he did leave his bank account— built up somewhat from pension checks — and his almost valueless East Texas farm near Telephone to his children and to me when he died a few years ago. But he lost the best friend he ever had at Mama's death. Lizzie, too, his second wife, was a very good friend and helpmate. She stuck by him through thick and thin — often cooking and washing dishes in a local cafe for their food. In a strange sort of half-hearted way, Brother always seemed a little ashamed of Lizzie's lack of education, her slovenly appearance, and filthy way of living. But he need not have been because we all loved Lizzie for herself and for her unselfish care of Robert as long as she lived.

Why did Mama do so much for Brother? Who knows? Perhaps it was just a normal mother's love for her son. Perhaps it was because he was the only man in her life. "Perhaps," (as she often confided to me when I would crawl into her Jenny Lind bed with her on a cold night) "he sort of takes the place of my father, my brother, and my husband."

What went on in her heart no one will ever know. Never, during the four remaining years of his life, had she spoken an accusing word to her father, who had been remanded to her custody. Never had she blamed Robert for being responsible for the tragedy that had changed her life. But a picture of my father, taken on the day he became County Clerk, always hung over the desk in the National Hotel.

To me, Bob was my big brother and he could do no wrong. He was the good-looking, dashing Prince Charming who made infrequent visits to our planet, always with stylish clothes, Stetson hat, new automobile — or else with watermelons or produce or chickens. He would perch for a short while on the outskirts of our lives and then fly off for some new adventure. He represented romance in my young life; and when he'd say: "Come climb on my knee and I'll tell you a tale of Booger County," I could have listened indefinitely.

I could just picture the way he looked when he stepped off a curb in Los Angeles, all decked out in his cowboy boots and western pants; a cop called out to him above the roar of traffic: "Hi! Texas."

I loved to hear Brother tell stories about people he had known. The one that topped them all was the story of Mr. Eldridge. He was an old man with very comical characteristics — chief among which was his chin whiskers. He also had the habit of adding "awh" to every statement he made. I've seen Bob actually wipe tears from his eyes as he would say: "Get down,

44

Bill," (his favorite nickname for me), "I've told you all the tales I can think of today----Awh", and his chin whiskers stood out— in perfect imitation of Mr. Eldridge.

When I think back over the professions my brother might have entered instead of leading his wandering, aimless life, I realize how he frittered away his talents.

He might have been a lawyer or politician had he devoted to those professions the time which he gave to animals or drunks. In a letter written to me, he once confessed "Yes, Ruth, I wish I had studied Latin more when I took it in high school." Goodness knows, Bob grew up in an atmosphere that was crowded with those influences in the county seat of Robertson County. Instead, he turned these leanings to being a deputy, or a member of a posse, or a prison guard. With his remembrance of detail, the charm of his voice, and his gift for being a raconteur, I feel sure that he could have been either a writer or speaker. Had he devoted his sense of timing, his accuracy, and his splendid physique to professional baseball (one of his minor loves) he might have been another Babe Ruth. I know he could have been a surgeon if he had given that same devotion for operating and healing to the human race rather than to dogs, horses, and cows!

Ah! the professions he might have excelled in had he not been haunted by a curse, pursued by demons, born under an unlucky star! Often enough had he confided to me, his little sister Ruth, his dreams and ambitions — and doubtings. He was willing to work hard, loved nature, had an infinite capacity for making friends and entertaining them; but he was to go through life never realizing his full potential. However, I am confident that he loved the life he lived.

Well, I guess I could just keep on writing about Brother for hours and hours; but there are lots of stories I want to tell about his children and my sister Jimmie's and my own daughter — born late in my life — and their relationship to Mama and to the National Hotel. So I shall end this dissertation with Brother's own words as he recorded them a few years ago on my tape recorder.

"Sitting here in my wheelchair in the Veteran's Hospital in Bonham, Texas, I contemplate on how Booger County got its name. It's a well known fact that old Robertson County, Texas, is known far and wide as *Booger County*. Why just a few years ago there were so many families from Robertson County living on one street in the metropolis of Houston that they put up signs in their yards reading *Booger County Avenue*.

"There was never but two men who knew the whole story of the renowned moniker of Robertson County; they were Ben Myatt and R. L. Rucker. Ben started the whole shootin' match being aided and abetted by myself.

"A little past the turn of the century, Ben was living out of Bremond where I went one summer to assist him with some dog training. While we were shootin' the breeze one night, he observed that 'tha time was ripe for a Booger scare.' So he set about making a Dumb Bull. A Dumb Bull is a man-made voice of a Booger, which Ben considered essential. I tried to do exactly like Ben. After some searching. I found a small hollow juniper tree, cut off about a three-foot length and stretched over it, drum-like, a piece of fresh or green cowhide. To make sure it was tight, I fastened it with a solid row of tacks. After it had completely dried, then I made a small hole in the center of the hide and ran a cord about half the size of a writin' pencil through the hole, down the hollow, and extendin' about two feet more. On the string was tied a small, strong stick to keep it from pullin' through the cowhide. Then I worked a heavy coat of rosin into the string. Ben called the contrivance his lion and when he would hold the string tight with one hand and grip the cord in the other hand, the resultant sawing noise — shrill or coarse — would sound like a real Booger. With a little practice on the string and the stick and the cord, I could produce a sonorous roar that would make the Ringling Brothers' lion sound like a pussy cat.

"The fear generated by the offensive sound soon spread among the habitants, people and livestock. On one occasion, an old Polander was driving a gentle old horse to a single buggy.

He thought he heard a noise, which he did. My lion just murmured a light "meow"; the driver stopped his horse. Then the lion belted out a pretty good bellow and the gentle old horse gave one powerful lunge forward and broke the shafts loose from the buggy, took off for the tail and undercut, and was not seen for a week.

"Occasionally, during the next several years, I would resurrect the Booger. Once a little old crazy locoed mule fell into a ravine about ten feet deep and killed itself. So, via the pocket knife, I made a few jabs in one shoulder where the Booger had held on with his claws and cut the mule's throat with his claws on the other foot. This convinced the country boys that the Booger had caught and killed him for sure. The Booger did not eat any flesh — just drank the mule's blood and left.

"It was this last touch which proved too much. The people in the neighborhood were literally scared to death. Their children had to walk to school down country roads, so dozens of families kept their kids at home or else moved out, lock, stock, and barrel.

"I could plainly see the handwritin' on the wall. The Booger had to go. Now he remains in name only. When you get a thing like that rollin', there's just no place to stop halfway; it keeps getting bigger and bigger 'til quittin' is the only way out. I hung the Dumb Bull forever on a nail behind the door, reluctantly cut the old lion's throat, and buried him—facin' [leaning slightly as the gun had leaned fifty years before] East."

RUTH

IV

"To tell sad stories of my own mishaps"

— *William Shakespeare*

With Emphasis on Verna Ruth Rucker Lemming Called Ruth or Aunt Ruth.

Difficulties! Difficulties! Difficulties! I encounter many of them as I try to write about myself. How nearly impossible it is to comment on a commentator! So I am finding it a hard task to write about myself in the same way that I write about others. But I am a part of this story; therefore I'll try.

An assignment I made to my speech students early each semester was to talk about the guiding principles of their lives. Well, at the risk of being misunderstood, I suppose I'd have to say that the guiding principle of my life is service to others. If I can help someone, I like to do it. There! I've said the hardest part to put into words; so let's get on with it!

I don't remember when we first came to the National Hotel that was to exert such a great influence on my life, but I do remember running away from my grandfather and into the open arms of my big brother, Robert, whenever I got into trouble. But he was a boy and could not understand the difficulties of being a girl, so I frequently turned to Mama whenever I could find her free for a moment. Even though she understood me better, her maturity gave me a grown up viewpoint that seemed to endow me with a wisdom far beyond my years.

So, somehow, I have always been grown. I never had time nor inclination to do and say childish things. I took on responsibilities and had few minutes to waste on juvenile pursuits. Athletic contests had no appeal for me; I never cared for jokes or humor; games were not fascinating. Not until I was grown and out on my own to make my way among my peers did I take the time for relaxation and play—but not in my childhood or young girlhood. Then, I assumed grown up characteristics such as standing on tiptoe to reach dishes up to the table, standing up on a chair behind the counter collecting from the drummers — and making change — to their everlasting satisfaction, eating a piece of chicken as I went rushingly back to school after running home to perform duties, taking care of younger children — serious care — feeling very much their Aunt Ruth. I took no thought of the pleasures of being young but only of the unfortunate ordeals of trying to be adult before my time.

I do not have too many memories of my girlhood, but I do remember that Mr. Silverman was always around and that Mama kept a mental tab on the time of day by the things he did. He always walked up the street about 9:30, visited Gilland Brothers' Store, talked with several people on the street, and then came back to the Hotel by 11:00. He would sit around in the lobby and talk with anyone else who might be there till it was lunch time. After eating, he'd go upstairs to take a nap. After he came back down he always rode me on his knee and told me about Mollie Bailey's Circus and her fourteen elephants. I took it all in—wide-eyed! And about once a week there were very few drummers at the hotel. Most of them either went to a bigger city or to their homes for the weekend. Mr. Silverman would take me into the holy of holies and *try* to teach me to play dominoes. Well, at least I had a good teacher! All the traveling men teased him about having a little black rulebook full of his domino tricks. They knew that the only two words he could read or write were ''Abe Silverman'' at the bottom of a check or legal document. But any one of them would have been proud to accept such a check.

They tell me I was a favorite with the drummers who patronized our hotel. When I was only four years old, Mama had taught me all of Longfellow's *The Village Blacksmith*. One of the men would pick me up and put me on the desk in the lobby of the hotel (which we called the ''office.'' Oh, how the division of the words in the front window fascinated me—HOT-EL—OFF-ICE.) ''Now then'', he'd say, ''Let's hear Little Ruth in *The Village Blacksmith.*" You may be sure that the nickels and dimes rained about my feet when I'd get to: "The muscles of his brawny arms are strong as iron bands."

One of the most wonderful times of my life was the summer Mama, Alys Truett and I took a trip to West Virginia. I got on the first boat I had ever been on in New Orleans and we sailed to New York. There Alys and Mama went out to hunt for a Baptist Church and left me at the hotel with a maid for a nurse. I had been sick since our ship landed, so I do not have many happy memories of the Big Apple. However, my memories of West Virginia, our picnics, our horseback rides, and visit to an old abandoned mine were much more vivid. Besides, I often had Connie to myself, to play with and care for — my very own niece! The first one I ever had! And to think that I got to bring her back to Texas with me.

Every Saturday morning, Mama would send me over to Peter Edward's negro cafe to buy some fish to serve at the hotel. This was a rare privilege, as Peter always bought a small barrel of fish once a week. While his wife, Lizzie, was getting my fish, I always played awhile with their two children. They were smart, very dear little girls who grew up to be schoolteachers.

Somehow, my friendship with Peter Edward's children, with Betty, our colored cook, with Aunt Fannie Porch, with our Polish cook, Morgan, my close relationship with Mr. Silverman and with the Blonstein boys, who were in my room at school, enabled me to grow up in a small Southern town without any prejudices of race, creed or color. But I will have to confess that some of the race riots the last few years, some of the wetback activities, and our practically open door policies to foreign refugees leave me cold.

A very interesting area in Franklin was the old Overall place which we passed several times a day on our way to town or school. It was located where the First State Bank is now. Mrs. Overall still lived there then, with her brother, Ed Linton, in a big old dilapidated house. It had been a resort and show place

51

when the mineral well had produced, but it had fallen on hard times after the water was discovered at Marlin. There were the remains of flowers in the strictly formal beds surrounding the grounds, and we would reach through the wrought iron fence and pick some to take to the teacher at school, who always put them in an empty ink bottle filled with water. We'd try to peep into the windows of the house, but they were too dust covered to see through. We were deathly afraid of Ed Linton who sometimes chased us down the street — with no bad intentions, however, merely guarding his sister's property. Poor Ed; he was mentally retarded; but we always thought the house was haunted.

The first swimming pool in Franklin was at Gum Branch where they'd build a dam each summer because the winter rains would wash out the dam. We had a separate boys' and girls' bathhouse to change clothes in. They had no roofs over them — just board sides with a door and steps leading down to the water. Minnie, I think, hated the home-made bathing suits more than any of Mama's children or grandchildren. One summer Mama made on her old treadle Singer sewing machine (which still sits in my middle room) bathing suits for all of us. They were made of blue serge, with long legs and short sleeves, red and white braid around the collars, and long over blouses. I am reminded of the first all rubber bathing suit seen in Franklin at Mr. Elmo Reynold's Variety Store. Minnie worked there on Saturdays, and she was such a favorite with him that he always gave her all sorts of things that were not selling well in the store. So she fell heir to this bathing suit which she managed to wear in swimming — once — before Mama saw it and made her throw it away. Mama would let us go swimming, but I had to rush home just about the time everybody else got there, to help with supper.

Sometimes a jury would stay overnight at the hotel. A deputy slept outside in the hall to see that no one communicated with the jury. We prepared and carried the noon meal to juries in the courthouse and to election holders in the library. What an interesting break that was in the regular routine of serving meals at the hotel. I'd open glass jars, put the food from hot containers into big bowls, and serve myriad glasses of iced tea, already sweetened, from the old churn that Mama had sent; it was kept for many years for the jury tea.

I was twelve when Jimmie came home to live with her two children — just the right age to take care of them as they grew up. First, Connie and Frances and then, soon Minnie and Robert. Four more for Mama to provide for. I was just enough older than the kids to have to care for them, but I loved every minute of it because I loved them all four dearly, and we grew up with a strange, sweet relationship to each other that put these words in Robert's mouth the day he graduated from Texas A&M: "You know, Aunt Ruth, you've always been a kind of combination mother-sister-sweetheart to me all my life."

When they were little, Aunt Ruth was the one who got up in the night to take them to the bathroom. I usually had to go myself. I was the one who rushed to get them ready to go to Sunday School or entertained them. One day we were at Louis Gray's playing baseball. Robert swallowed a dime. I ran all the way home carrying him upside down trying to shake out the dime. In answer to my frantic cries, Mama came running out the back door, grabbed Robert and beat him on the back; and up came the coin.

We were never embarrassed about doing any of the hotel chores. We would empty the tall Betsys and clean them out, change the beds and sweep the floors. Mama lived by the philosophy: "Sufficient unto the day is the evil thereof," and we never felt that we had a hard row to hoe. Nor did we feel that any task was menial. They were just jobs that had to be done, and besides there was always the next night. As Mr. Silverman said, "Another day, another dollar."

One night there was a big fire in Franklin. All the stores from Mitchell's corner down to the hotel garden were burning. Gigantic flames leapt toward the sky. It looked as bad to me as the T.V. pictures of the Woodway Apartments fire in July,

1979, in Houston. Men pulled quilts (most of which were made by Mama's hands) from beds, wet them, and placed them up on our roof to repel the sparks which were flying everywhere. People formed bucket brigades which passed buckets, bowls, pitchers, any type of containers, full of water down the line and saved many buildings thereby. I carried mattresses out frantically to the pitiful clumps of furniture assembled in the yard. One boy and I carried our piano out and down the front steps. Fright can do wonders. (Like the illustration I often used in speech classes about the Negro man near Houston who seemed to have super-human powers to lift a car off the ground in order to save the life of a white man trapped beneath the burning wreckage.)

The four kids were awakened in the middle of the night, each one wrapped in a blanket, and taken to a nearby ditch. They didn't dare to move, in repsonse to my quoted orders from Mama, while I carried out mattresses and pianos. After the fire was extinguished, I took them up to Aunt Nan's where they slept on the floor on their blankets. Robert, now a professor-emeritus from Texas A & M, said to me recently: "I don't remember anything about the fire. All I can recollect is that we had only cornflakes for breakfast served with milk fresh from the cow. I ate a whole box of cornflakes." Strange how things like that stay in one's memory!

I can remember so many of the drummers who used to come to the hotel — weekly, monthly, or even semi-annually. They had favorite rooms, and they were always greeted as old friends, usually asking for Abe when they first arrived.

Miss Axtell was a visitor who came once a year for several years. Her nephew Dick was investing in land all over Texas and had one plot near Franklin. She was a sparse New Englander with a decided English accent. Her usual attire was a long black taffeta skirt topped by a crisp white long-sleeved blouse. A little gold watch which she wore pinned over her heart always fascinated me. Miss Axtell stayed long enough one summer to have a china painting class with some of the children in town. I was rather small to take lessons, but she often let me join them anyhow. I can still remember her saying: "Now girrrrrrls, you must observe the flowers carefully and paint in every *leaf* and *petal* on your plates.''

Miss Axtell gave me a child's hand painted china tea set which became one of my most prized possessions. I almost took it to college with me. Once when I came home from college, I found that Mama had let the children play with it and with all my playthings and that the whole tea set was broken except for one little handleless cup. I cried over it a little, but I could not remain angry long because I was so glad to see them all and they were my very own charges — my own nieces and newphew and could therefore do no wrong. They were too young to realize its value to me. But that little cup, with the broken handle, went everywhere with me that I have ever lived: Elgin, Lott, Calvert, Bryan, California, Washington, Oklahoma, Tyler, Temple, Bryan, Wharton, Houston. It now occupies a prominent place on the black whatnot shelf that Uncle Polk had handmade for me so many years ago. The little Dutch girl is still feeding the swan — all alone, just one little girl who lost all her companions on the other broken dishes. I am reminded of Keats' *'Ode On A Grecian Urn* —

''A thing of beauty is a joy forever.''

Mama was an ardent WCTUer and later a prohibitionist, but she would occasionally have a glass of brother's home brew beer and she made a bowl of eggnog every Christmas for the family. This was one of the contradictions in Mama's nature. So naturally I thought of her when a group of boys and girls wanted to go up to Mildred's to make some eggnog one Christmas afternoon. Mildred had taught school several years at that time, and I had been to college two years and I had taught school one year. So I don't believe there was a question of our maturity. Besides, we already had the nog.

I offered: ''O.K. if none of you young people know how to make eggnog, I'll go straight to headquarters and find out.'' So I asked Mama how to make it.

Her response was: ''Now, Ruthie, you know I don't believe in drinking — and, for certain not in boys and girls drinking

55

together. I know that if Mrs. Beall was living she wouldn't approve of you doing that. Liquor is one arm of the devil ----------'' and so on for about ten minutes.

Then Mama proceeded to tell me exactly how to make it!

Mama was always interested in politics and one of her pet peeves was Jim Ferguson. Once he came to Franklin campaigning for governor; a room had been reserved for him at the National Hotel. Mama discovered that I had put a poster advertising his opponent on the wall of his room. She made me take it down. I did what she told me, but I managed to find a poster of Jim to take its place; on his picture I drew a moustache.

Mama and I had a very close relationship. I nearly always went home and told her everything that had happened at an important or unimportant occasion that I went to. But I felt differently the first time a boy asked to walk home with me. Besides, I had already figured out my answer to his request to kiss me goodnight. When he said: ''There's nothing wrong with it,'' I would answer: ''There's nothing right with it either.'' So I was quite humiliated when he just brought me to the edge of the porch in front of the sample room, turned without a word, and ran back up the street.

When I got in the house, Mama's questions were particularly irksome. ''How many boys were there? How many girls? What games did you play? Who had to pay forfeits? Was the hostess' mother in the room with you? What did they have for refreshments?''

I had managed to answer all her questions fairly and honestly. However, I became more irritated with each query. Then she came out with the $64,000 question: ''Who was that little boy who walked home with you?''

I had become thoroughly indignant by this time so I blurted out: ''I--I--I think it was John Steele.''

Never did I live this down. Even after I was grown, Mama would occasionally ask me: ''Well, Ruthie, who do you *think* the boy was that you went out with tonight?''

The children all loved for me to read to them. I read *Five Little Peppers and How They Grew* and *Anne of Green Gables* aloud so many times that I almost knew them by heart. Frances would always fall asleep in the middle of my reading and then wake up with a start. Despite her begging, no one would tell her a thing about the part she had missed.

I got in the habit of saving all the place cards, decorations, and favors of everything I went to, particularly while I was in college. I did not have much money to spend on presents, so I tried to share things with the four kids. They would all sit around with wide opened eyes and hands when Aunt Ruth would come home. I brought them such momentos as ribbons, tassels, napkins (even used ones), and printed programs (which I summarized for them — with gestures.) Then I would apportion them out to the four who kept and cherished them reverently.

Children nowadays have so many gifts for Christmas. Our children always hung up their stockings and I played Santa Claus and had great fun filling them. But they did not get great multitudes of expensive gifts such as children do now. They would get a piece or two of fruit — an apple or an orange, maybe some candy and nuts; a small present or two such as a comb and brush or mirror, a book, a small toy, Flinch cards with red roses on them; and then perhaps one real gift such as a doll, a picture, a purse, or a little train. But they loved all the things very much and treasured and played with them for years.

When I was 16 years old, Mama sent me to Baylor College Academy. She explained her reasons to Mr. Silverman thus:

"Ruth never had any real childhood. She's always had somebody to take care of; and I'm not going to have her take care of my poor Sister Sally who is coming to live with us. She has rheumatoid arthritis, and is almost an invalid. I want Ruth to have a chance to live life joyfully and be carefree while she's still a girl. Besides, I don't want her to waste a year. She only has to make two more credits to be a high school graduate, and she can take her Freshman work in college at the same time." Mr. Silverman understood this reasoning. It was economic. So off I went — joyfully, despite changing trains in Milano at night.

57

I spent four of the happiest years of my life in Baylor College — although I had to overcome a very bad case of homesickness for my family and hotel life.

College was much the same for me as it was for any girl in the '20s. The rules were strict; the activities were excellent; the classes opened new worlds for me; and the associations were wonderful. I shall try to give two examples of each of these to help explain why after more than 50 years I can still sing: "Old Baylor, dear Baylor, My heart clings to thee."

One would have to begin with rules, for they were very rigid about behavior on Sundays. We were herded like sheep and made to march downtown to church. We had sack lunches given to us at noon for supper that night which we always ate about 2 or 3 o'clock and then suffered from hunger the rest of the time, unless someone had recently received a box from home or had a bunch of candy bars.

But my sin was that I had dared to ask if I could go riding with Alice Evans and her parents from Franklin who had driven over to see us one Sunday afternoon. I didn't have written permission from Mama to go, so Mrs. Ely refused to sign my permit. As we went out into the hall I sobbed, "I'm not going to stay in this rotten place another day. I'm going home tomorrow." Mrs. Ely overheard me and called me back to her room where I had to stay for an hour, on my knees, praying to the Lord to forgive me. You'd better believe that Mama sent me a blanket permission to go out with anyone I wanted to from that time on.

Mama, always alert to new things, rented Miss Mamye McCoy the parlor of the hotel for a week one summer vacation to give the new permanent waves with a big electric machine. She gave Frances a free one for demonstration. There were tight little curls all over her head, which Frances thought were beautiful. I decided to get one too before going back to Baylor in the fall. Miss Mayme had finished rolling up my hair. She had put the clamps on and had just turned on the electricity; then something happened; the electricity went off! There was nothing to do but wait. Some men came over from Hearne to work on it; they got it back on late that afternoon. I entertained all the customers and hotel guests in the meantime by reciting reams of poetry. The results of my first permanent were not too satisfactory, and for the next several months I usually wore a big bandana to hide the frizz on my head.

I must digress even more for a moment here to tell about the very first permanent wave ever given in Franklin several years previously. Mama had rented out two rooms to the travelling ladies who advertised the wonderful discovery. Minnie was only ten years old, but she desperately wanted a permanent. Brother found her crying in the ironing room.

"Come on, Kooter. Tell Daddy what's the matter."

Minnie sobbed: "I am tired of having my hair rolled up on a string so it will be curly."

"For God's sake, Mama; let her get a permanent wave if she wants it."

So Mama yielded to the argument that the cost of the wave would be taken out of the room rent and Minnie got her heart's desire. It took all day, but she loved it. She promised herself that she would never do without a permanent again if she had to scrub floors to pay for it, and so far as I know, she never has.

The other story I shall tell is about the Sunday night a bunch of us were so hungry that we just couldn't stand it, so we went to Mrs. Ely's private garden behind the dormitory to try to swipe a few vegetables. We were vigorously pulling up some green onions when a bright light flashed on us. It was Mrs. Ely holding a flashlight. We ran fleetly around the dorm and into the front door, Mrs. Ely in hot pursuit. We had the presence of mind to run to the bathroom on the second floor and flush the onions down the toilet. And we were sound asleep in our beds on the third floor with the cover pulled up tightly when Mrs. Ely went from room to room to check the girls. I feel compelled to say that the next day they had to get a plumber to unstop two commodes on the second floor.

In my listing above I said the activities were excellent. I will leave out all the superior religious groups, everything connected with student government and class offices, the literary societies (which took the place of sororities and fraternities) and all the numerous class and social activities with which our campus teemed and I will talk a little bit about the two activities which meant the most to me — the Debate Squad and the Choral Club.

I got into debate almost by accident, and somehow found the square peg that fitted the square hole. My deep interest in public affairs, my love of research, and my knowledge of some of the principles of logical reasoning stem from this association. Two years I won the college debate pin. I took many wonderful trips, had the privilege of knowing, personally, the debate coach, Dr. Vann, with the richness that he brought to my life, got to work with and know the president's daughter, Martha Hardy, with Alma Lee Joiner and Cora Whitley, and all the wonderful bunch of girls who participated in debate, and was a charter member of Phi Theta Kappa and helped to win the national championship.

The other activity in which I wanted to put my best foot forward was the Choral Club. With Mrs. Allie Coleman Pierce as director, we sang at many affairs both on and off the campus and took a tour each year, two weeks away from the campus, and the entertainment was royal. The only fly in the ointment was that I always had to wear a white evening dress that my mother had hand made. I thought that everyone else was wearing a store-bought dress. I'm sure that this was the guiding principle behind my buying my daughter a black ready-made evening dress for fifty dollars when she was only a Junior in high school. That and the fact that I could not possibly have made one at all — much less with the loving stitches which Mama had put in mine.

At Baylor I grew up mentally, emotionally, and spiritually. Most of the beauty and inspiration of my life came to me there. I gained 25 pounds in weight and I learned so many wonderful things in my classes. I was very busy and happy, particularly in Dr. William Harvey Vann's Shakespeare and modern poetry classes and — and — and oh! everything that Dr. Billy Vann taught. After my freshman English, every course I took in

English was taught by Mr. Billy in his own inimitable style. That's the reason why my English major had 15 extra hours that did not count on my degree. No person, other than my mother, had a greater influence on my life and interests. Not a day passed while I was teaching that I did not quote him.

Mr. Vann gave me a leather bound copy of Shakespeare's plays in which he wrote the inscription: "To Ruth Rucker on the occasion of her second unanimous victory." This I shall treasure for all my life. My love for modern poetry was established in his class, although the word *modern* has changed much in meaning during my life span.

My senior year was no more than started, when Dean Townsend sent for me one day and said, "Why, Ruth Rucker, you have never even taken your Freshman course in chemistry." I tried to explain to him how I was a senior in the Academy that year, but nothing would do him but that I must drop one English course I was registered for and take chemistry so that I would graduate that year. Little did he know what a horror science was to me. My teacher gave ten questions on every exam, seven of them were on the textbook and three were originals. I made a straight 70 on his exams — never even attempted an original. Luckily, Dickie Adams, one of my best friends, was an art major, and my notebook in chemistry was filled with beautiful drawings of things I was supposed to have seen when I looked into the microscope.

Miss Edith Roper taught me trig. On the outside of my midterm exam, together with a grade of 20, was written her admonition: "Miss Rucker, it seems you are failing the course." Well, I never had failed one and so I dropped Choral Club and Debate the rest of that year and memorized the trig book. Luckily, Miss Roper did not change any wording in the final she gave or I would never have made the 100. This time she wrote: "Miss Rucker, you have a real mathematical brain. I'd like to see you major in math." I tell these two tales about math and science to explain the 2 C's on my undergraduate record. Luckily, Mama had never put me under any pressure to make specific grades — only to pass.

The last point in my list concerned the wonderful associations that were found in Baylor. I do not have time to catalog all of them, besides, they do not really belong in this book, but they were numerous and invaluable to me. I will mention only a few. First came Dickie Adams who was my best pal. So little was she that she could walk under my outraised arm. We were the Mutt and Jeff of the campus. Corinne Vercer, my senior roommate, Georgia Westbrook, Martha Hardy and oh so many more! I was elected Senior Class President in *absentia*. I received a wire from Georgia stating: "Ruth Rucker will be our Senior Class President." The one from Martha read: "Proud of our Senior Class President. Glad she is my Academia sister." Memories of how we took Miss Osee Maedgen under our wing and taught her the Baylor traditions. She was our special property, since she had come to Baylor to marry our Mr. Vann. And Olyvya Long! We suffered together through almost every play that Miss Walters and Miss Lattimer gave for four years. We spent the night before graduation recounting tales of them and of our undying friendship as we sat on a patchwork quilt made by my mother on a spot on "Old Baylor's dear soil" behind Alma Reeves chapel.

Reluctantly, I pass on from my college life. All the reminders of this will have to be told in much less detail because it is not closely related to the National Hotel.

I am going to skip several very eventful years to tell a few things about the four summers I went to Northwestern University. Mama was still living at the National Hotel. Brother's children were growing to maturity under her guidance, and Sister and her girls were married to Archie Smith and living in several different places. Need I say that Mama strongly encouraged me to go to school further. I looked into the various schools that offered a Master's Degree in Speech and Drama and found that there were only five in the United States that did at that time — none of which were in Texas. Besides, Chicago did not seem so very far away and Northwestern was an excellent school. So I went up — really on an exploratory trip to see if I could afford to go there.

I was really the country girl gone to town when I arrived in

Chicago, after traveling day and night for 48 hours on a bus from Waco. I checked my bags in the station and went out to find my way out to Evanston via the elevated train. I'll not tell much about the first day except to say that I tramped all day long and could not find a place that was not too expensive. So, in desperation, I returned to 1838 Chicago Avenue, just across the street from the main campus at Northwestern University. The nice lady who ran the place was a Tennesseean and had asked me to come back and spend the night as her guest if I had not found a room; I had to report that I could not afford any which I had found.

When I knocked on her door, she met me cheerfully and said: "Come in, my dear. I thought of something after you left this morning that might suit you. I'd so love to have you." Then she took me upstairs. The house had originally been intended for a three-story house, but the third floor had never been completed. She preceeded me up the second winding stairs that led to the incomplete third floor. There, in one corner, was a bed, chest of drawers, and a drop light. Adjoining was a shower and a commode — nothing more. "In the winter I give this room to the boy who maintains my furnace and keeps my yard. No one has ever stayed up here in the summer, but I guess you won't mind the heat, since you're from Texas. I can rent this to you for $10.00 a week — if you want it. Stay awhile and think it over. I must go put the blueberry muffins in the stove for our supper."

What more could I have asked for? I had a comfortable place to sleep, a good light, a place to bathe, privacy to eat some meals direct from the grocery store and all the rafters and cobwebs and dormer windows one could have desired to practice my speeches on. One wonderful thing about the location was that it was only five blocks from downtown Evanston. I could walk to the weekly speech luncheons at the Orrington Hotel where I developed friendships with Lew Sarett, Carl Sandburg and Edgar Bergen. I could buy a pretty fair lunch at Woolworth's for 15¢ and thereby save more money for my weekly trip to the city to hear Cab Calloway or Sophie Tucker or to see Sally Rand or John Barrymore. I fell in love with my garret

63

and was able to stay there all four summers I attended Northwestern.

I shall relate only a few happenings from the list of 15 or more I have made out. Isn't it strange that we know more about ourselves than we remember about others. That little nugget of wisdom makes me wonder whether I was right when I wrote down the guiding principle of my life about 18 pages ago. The first incident happened the day after I had gone into Chicago and brought back my possessions which I had to take up the little winding steps one at a time.

I was one of the first students admitted to Dean Dennis' office after 8:00 a.m. and the very last one to leave — finally — about 6:00 p.m. Not that I spent the entire day talking to him, but that I was the most persistent. We were discussing the status of my degree from Baylor College in Belton, Texas. His argument was that Baylor was not a member of the American Association of Colleges and that I would have to take 60 semester hours in Northwestern to prove my degree. Mine, on the other hand, was that Baylor was a member of the Southern Association for geographic reasons and that in one summer's work at Northwestern I would be able to demonstrate whether I could do their work. (In that way I would be able to get my Master's in four summers.) I think he finally gave up in desperation because it was almost six o'clock in the afternoon when he said:

"Miss Rucker, I have never had a student to be so persistent. Here is what I have decided. Take the three courses which I have registered you for this summer semester, and if you make an A in all three of them, I will admit you as a candidate for a Master's Degree next summer."

My reply was: "Dean Dennis, will you put that in writing at the bottom of my transcript, please."

"Oh, you don't trust me," he ejaculated.

"No sir," I replied. "It has taken me too long to convince you this time. I don't want to have to do it again." So you can imagine that the days had to stretch to have more than 24 hours in them for me to study hard enough to make those three A's.

Little did he know of the indomitable spirit which I had inherited from Minnie Rucker — the spirit that had led a woman recently widowed by the inadvertant killing of her husband by her father to go into a business that a woman just did not enter then — and with no word of blame for her father. To make a success of that business and to make a respected place for herself, for her children, and for her grandchildren in a small town hotel was her ambition.

The other incident dealt with my oral exam, the finale of my work at the end of summer number four. Dr. Cunningham, my wonderful adviser, and I had studied and drilled over *all* the work I had taken at Northwestern. There was a board composed of four PH.D.'s with Dean Dennis as chairman. I was somewhat dejected that the two men from outside the Speech Department were from the History Department instead of being English teachers. I had had only the required courses in history, about 12 years before, while I had had all the English courses Dr. Vann taught and I had been teaching high school English myself for several years. But my thesis subject had seemed to indicate that history was my second subject; it was *Woodrow Wilson's Concept of American Principles as Expressed in His Speeches,* so I was given two history men.

Dr. Cunningham warned me about Dean Dennis' usual attitude: "Why, he'll be just as nice as peaches and cream, but look out. He is sure to spring something on you when you least expect it." I have always been glad that I was somewhat prepared for his question.

Well, we had had a very pleasant little conversation — the four men and I. One of the history men had asked me something about Patrick Henry which I was able to handle, as he had played a prominent part in *The History and Literature of American Oratory,* a speech course which I had taken the preceding summer. Then, there came a question on Lincoln which I had not been able to handle quite so successfully because it dealt with history completely. Things were quiet for a

65

minute; then Dean Dennis leaned forward across the table. "This is it," I reflected.

"Miss Rucker, what is your opinion of the Freudian principles?" I thought hard for a minute. Then I somehow managed to come up with the following answer:

"You threw me there for a minute, Dean. In the first place, down in Texas we say *Frood* not *Froid;* and in the second place, I'd rather discuss them with you on some moonlit night without the presence of all these witnesses."

Well, that brought the house down. Those men did more than laugh. They guffawed. And Dr. Cunningham had to wipe his glasses. The Dean asked me to step out in the hall for a minute, and a few seconds later they called me back in and shook hands with me in congratulation and said that they had each one signed his name in approval on my thesis. Less than one hour spent on my orals which usually took three hours!

After I was sure that the exams were over and all the men had signed my thesis, my mind turned to the Dixie Dinner in downtown Chicago to which I had been invited for that day. I had not accepted on account of the exam, but I was ready to go somewhere to celebrate. So I hied me to the El and went in past the sordid slums and the brave little geranium plants on fire escapes to the hotel where the dinner was to be held on the roof garden. I got off the elevator and the first person I saw was Dean Dennis.

"Why, Miss Rucker, what are you doing here?" he asked me.

"Where else would a Texas gal go to celebrate passing her orals?" I responded.

"If you had told me you were coming, you could have ridden down with me. I was invited to this dinner, also, because I was born in Kentucky."

Nothing would do him but an extra chair should be brought and placed at the head table next to him, for I found that he was to be M.C. at the dinner. He introduced me to the entire group and told the story about how I confounded the four PH.D.'s that very morning and passed my orals in record time. Quite a celebration!

66

I'm going to leave all the details of my marriage out of this book. They really have no place in it — save for one thing that Mama wrote her niece, Vance, in a letter which Vance gave to me after Mama's death.

"My baby girl, Ruth, has gone to Washington to live with her new husband. It nearly killed me to give Ruth up, but I could not deny her this little bit of happiness when she had been so good to me."

And I was happy — for an all too short time. Lem was a free soul. He could not stand to be fettered. The trauma of Jean's birth and my subsequent illness coupled with the lack of money and his honest efforts to be a good husband — plus his absolute inability to cope with it all — contributed to my decision to come back to Texas with my little daughter where we could begin life over again. I have no word of blame for Lem, only a vast loneliness for his dearness, his companionship and a deep sense of anguished regret for Jean's never seeing him or knowing him. I think she would have understood.

I have mentioned Mama's wandering foot previously. I think it must have been inherited by her peripatetic daughter. It must have been the gypsy in me that made me long to journey to specific places, to others not so exact, and just to ramble anywhere. The man who invented guide books was my best friend. I have numberless ones on file. The scrapbooks of all the trips I've taken fill the shelves in my big walk-in closet.

I used to lie awake in my little bed at the hotel in Franklin and listen to the I and GN trains passing through on the way to somewhere different and entrancing. There was one which came through about 4:30 every morning that had a particularly lonesome yet inviting whistle as it rolled on and on to some far-away place. The sound of its wheels seemed to hum over and over the words of a song we sang in school that day.

> "Oh beautiful for spacious skies,
> For amber waves of grain,
> For purple mountain majesties,
> Above the fruited plain."

67

As much as time and money would permit, I have followed the call of those turning wheels—followed to most of the states in America, to Canada, Alaska, the Caribbean, Hawaii and Mexico. I've been to most of the capitals of Europe, the Orient, Japan and China, Australia, the Fiji Islands. I've lived in the towns of Franklin, Belton, Elgin, Calvert, Bryan, Tyler, Temple, Wharton, Houston; in the States of Texas, Illinois, Oklahoma, California and Washington. I've traveled by car, by bus, train, sea and air. The rolling waves on *Hawaii 5-0* every week make me want to go to hundreds more. As my travel buddy, Oleane White, says: "You don't have to say *where* to me; just say *when?"*

I still have the same spirit and desires about travelling; its "clarion call" still comes clear, but conditions now seem to forbid my answering it affirmatively. I had planned to travel extensively when I retired. But alas for "the best laid plans o' mice and men", this plagued arthritis and general malaise of 76 years now interfere somewhat. I sit and look back through my old scrapbooks, attempt to put a few feelings down on paper, and go across to *The World Wide Health Studio* in an earnest attempt to improve both plights so that I may get back to my former intentions.

Often, I am reminded of the summer that Mama went with me on the bus to Chicago, and I got to share with her some of the wonders of the city I had come to love. At the age of 60, Mama had lost none of her enthusiasm for travel.

I may not have communicated to you how great is my true itinerant nature. One has to possess it himself before he can understand it in others. Like the two French sailors Jean and I walked behind one night in Tivoli Gardens in Copenhagen. They were trying to pick up a couple of Danish girls. They had tried in several languages, but to no avail. Finally one of them said in English: "Hello Baby, would you like to see some of the sights of the carnival with us?" To which one of the Danish girls replied: "Oh, boy, would we?" And after communication had been established, they walked away laughing, in *couples,* to see the acrobats.

My retirement in 1972 marked the end of 45 years of teaching. Now I get quite a nice retirement income plus social security as well. I am not going to write anything about this, the main part of my life, since it is not directly related to my life in the National Hotel. But I will say that I do consider teaching as one of the most valuable and rewarding professions in the world. I have touched the lives of many students who have gone on and into every branch of society and like Alexander Pope's character, I am glad that many of them have surpassed the teacher.

As I try to close this section, I look back over my life to find the prevailing characteristic. Perhaps you might not agree, but I believe it is my interest in Speech and Drama.

From the time we were little children, we had put on plays of our own composing in Room No. 17, at the end of the front and back porches. This was our sample room. It contained only long tables which could, in a pinch, be used for stage elevations or even for audience seats. We charged 10 pins for admission. I was always the combination author, director and general flunkey for the productions.

As I said, this room was ordinarily used for a sample room. The drummers would bring the things they had for sale in big packing boxes which Robert would carry across the street from the depot for many a 25¢ tip. Maybe that was the reason he felt so at ease and was the champion actor in our company. Here they would display their wares and bring in merchants from Franklin and nearby communities to see them. Now, in 1981, they have things in a truck and just go by each store for 15 or 20 minutes and then on to some big city for the night. Hotel business in a small town is not what it used to be.

Once a year a traveling company of actors came to Franklin with a tent show. This was the most exciting time of year for me. The members of the cast all stayed at the hotel, and you cannot imagine the thrill of seeing an actor play a demanding love role on the stage the night before, and then finding out that he wants soft boiled eggs to eat for breakfast the next morning. It was strange how many girls in Franklin decided that Ruth was one of their best friends and came down to see me, of course on the off chance that they would see a glamorous star or heroine.

At the tent, their show always had three acts. And between acts they would sell popcorn and peanuts and bottled pop. They usually played old-fashioned melodramas or westerns. I heard them talk shop at the hotel, and I became more and more interested. I was a favorite with them and they were amazed with the amount of poetry I could quote.

I can fully credit my decision to major in Speech to Miss Katherine Hurt of the Hurt School of Expression in Dallas whose slogan was *The Hurt School, But It Don't*. She came to Franklin and gave a recital at the Methodist Church. She stayed at the hotel and I had several private talks with her. One of the numbers on her repertoire was Amy Lowell's *Patterns*. It was the most beautiful, rhythmic and sensuous poem I had ever heard and I took a solemn vow then that I would learn to read that poem as well as Miss Hurt did. I don't think I ever succeeded, but after majoring in Speech and Drama for both my B.A. and M.A. degrees, and after teaching other students to speak for 45 years, I at least have tried.

Miss Ivy Hathaway taught us private expression lessons in Franklin and we put on plays and gave concerts. Once we even did a musical play *The Stars and Stripes Forever,* featuring Cicero McPhail. "Uncle Sam Stands With Flag Unfurled Before The Eyes of the World." I remember that Mildred said, *Under the Buggy Seat.* My favorite was *Ring for Liberty*. Miss Ivy taught in the Carnegie Library building. Chautauquas were a favorite form of entertainment lasting for two or three days. There would be a variety of imported talent, some singers, musicians, lecturers. We also had a Lyceum series of four or five numbers per year. Both of these performed in the library building. The artists always stayed at the hotel, so I got a double exposure to them. The courthouse was on the way to school, and I'm afraid that I frequently cut classes to listen to trials and to my favorite lawyer's speeches. Oh, speech was always in my background!

In most of the plays I was in at college, I had to play the part of a man, because I went to an all girls school and I was tall and adaptable vocally. We produced *The Taming of the Shrew, Twelfth Night, A Night at an Inn* and others too numerous to mention. I was in two or three major productions each year and on numerous programs for various clubs and organizations. When I started teaching I always directed three or four plays every year. I have been cast in various shows in Tyler, Temple, Wharton and once I was in a play at the Alley Theatre in Houston. The play was Jewel Gibson's *Joshua Beene and God.* How much she has enriched my life. Don't ask me how I came in from Wharton every night for rehearsals and performances for several weeks. But it was great.

I usually produced rather old standard plays such as *I Remember Mama, The Rainmaker, The Rocking Chair, White Iris, Our Town,* and *The Man Who Came To Dinner.* I felt that it was better for my students to be in really good plays even if they were old ones than to be in trashy ones; also, the royalties were not so high as on newer plays. I have found that plays give you wonderful relief from the every day trials of life. Each play is a challenge and a very wholesome and worthwhile pursuit for any number of students. I always felt that Mama understood my problems, motives and desires in putting on a play. They were the same ones she had tried to give me all of my life: "Give it all you've got, Ruthie; all your abilities, talents and enthusiasms. Then you have won success with each production."

A play "holds the mirror up to nature" in the words of Shakespeare. I loved the plays we gave. It was my theory, always, to bring good entertainment to the towns where I taught. I was interested in putting on a good show as well as in giving training to the students. So I have always tried to spread my influence to both areas—behind the floodlights and in front of the footlights, remembering the old adage:

The show must go on!

71

FRANCES AND CONSTANCE

V

"I'm off to see ----------"

— *Judy Garland*

The Wizard of Management — With Emphasis on Constance Merle
Garrett Galloway, Called Connie.

It is quite fitting that this chapter should be numbered *Five*
because Mama had five grandchildren, although her great heart
was full of love for all children. She had much influence, too, on
several of her great-grandchildren; but it was on these five that
the National Hotel (through its owner, Mrs. Minnie Rucker) exerted the greatest influence. They were as nearly her own as
grandchildren could ever be. The oldest four of them lived the
early part of their lives in Franklin, under the influence of the
National Hotel through good times and bad.

They lived an average life, albeit an un-average one. A life
almost devoid of men. It was a truly matriarchal society, one
dominated by Mama and her ideas. Only occasionally was
Brother around; he betook himself outside the cocoon. Just one
small boy, Robert, plagued and bantered the girls unmercifully
— his sister Minnie being his special tease and love — even when
he called her "Minnie Marie" after a girl who was not quite "all
there." Some hotel guests were influential; occasional relatives
and friends passed through their lives; but fundamentally, they
lived in a state of Mom-ism. We have all been governed by this
double implementation of a life in which women were forced to
be the breadwinners, the workers, the independents, the decision makers, the doers.

My sister, Jimmie, had two girls: Constance and Frances;
they came to the National Hotel to live, even before the birth of
Frances. As often as not, Constance was known as Connie and

Frances was known as Bucky. Connie was jolly, ladylike, well behaved. Her childish name for her sister was Bucky. I remember a picture we took on the front porch. Connie was sitting decorously quiet with the ribbon tied in flat bows on her crocheted cap so carefully made by Sister's ever busy hands. But not Frances. She was sitting astride the bannisters with her cap awry and with a piquant expression on her face. The same look with which she asked a drummer: "Have you got a nickel, just a itty-bitty nickel?" and when the victim had replied favorably she countered: "Connie and Robert and Minnie want one too." Thus was born her lifelong habit of looking after those she loved.

Connie's arrival on this planet was awaited as eagerly in Texas as in West Virginia. One May morning, Mama received a telegram signed "Frank" and reading "Greetings to Grandmother, a girl." Mama took her cane, grabbed her shawl, jerked her head high and walked up and down the streets of Franklin, showing off the wire and proudly telling everyone: "Jimmie had a girl!"

When she went to West Virginia to visit the Garretts, she was very happy to be with her first-born grandchild and she was more than happy — although she worried considerably about Frank — when they came to Texas to live. She opened her heart and the National Hotel to them, particularly to Connie, although I cannot really say that Mama had a favorite. Each child had his or her own place — even to the special niche occupied by my daughter, Jean, after Mama was no longer in the hotel. But its influence flourished as long as she lived, and it flowered in all of us — even long after she was gone. But I started (before my usual habit of rambling on broke in) to write about Mama's grandchildren in some semblance of order; so here goes.

Everyone liked Connie from childhood to maturity. She was a happy, outgoing child, with her father's disposition, even though his looks were inherited by Frances. She often sat on the fence which encircled the hotel yard and waved to the train men as they passed. They all knew her and enthusiastically waved back at the friendly little lady.

74

The children played on the street going to the post office, and one day Connie, who was just about four, came home without her sweater. Sister directed her to go back to look for it. Connie was afraid to go after dark and complained: "Those old boys will throw rocks at me." Frances stepped into the breach, "Come on, Sister. I'll go with you and I'll cock 'em down."

We children often played in No. 17, a big room at the end of the porch where the drummers laid out their samples; we would arrange a screen and pull a blanket or sheet, sometimes a towsack, for the curtain. I was always the combined author-director and Robert had to take all the male roles. One of our favorites was *The Sleeping Beauty,* with Connie as the beauty and Robert as Prince Charming. He awakened her with a kiss, a resounding smack, which was just as often a bite or a smothered giggle. The admission to these dramatic efforts was ten pins, as I have said before.

The children played numerous games. Sometimes I played with them, but as often as not, I was somewhere "sucking a book" as Mama put it, because that was the thing I loved most. One of their favorite games was Jacks, making up new and strange versions as time went on. I still remember the pandemonium that occurred the day Connie crawled over the floor in search of a runaway Jack. She found it all right — by sticking one of the prongs into her knee. We were all too scared to be punished.

There was a streetlight in the corner of the hotel yard, so at night they would all four play with the Andrews children from across the street. One of their preferred games was "Wolf Over the River"; another was "Statues"; and sometimes they would be so bold as to play "Annie Over" and throw a ball clear over the hotel. Connie was the ringleader in these games.

Sister and her children always had the room behind the parlor. The children thought it was heavenly to have their own private telephone hanging on the wall. They did not realize that the telephone company for which Jimmie worked required it. The phone in the little booth in the lobby of the hotel might be busy when they needed to call her.

In this room they were a family. Connie says that Jimmie would know what they were doing or saying — even with her back turned to them as she stood at the ironing board or sat at the sewing machine. But the room was full of love and shared confidences. Connie remembers sleeping in the bed with her mother the very first Christmas Eve that she knew there was no Santa Claus. Of course, I had been the official Santa Claus — never really being a child again after they had come to live with us. There was a feeling of camaraderie, an innate sense of togetherness and an aura of happiness emanating from their room. This was a feeling which I coveted.

After they moved to the apartment at Miss Ella's and then to the house near the standpipe, the girls would come down to the hotel and work. Mama always had to have someone to wait on the tables, and Connie and Frances certainly knew the business. Besides, there was usually some leftover chicken or a pot of soup that Mama could send home by the girls even though actual cash was mighty scarce. So Connie had learned at an early age to manipulate and manage despite hardships.

During the war years, everyone had a special task to do. Connie still remembers that hers was to watch the sugar bowls to see that no one took away any extra sugar. Too bad that was before the day of individual packets doled out by the waitress. This task Connie managed to do — just the way she has always managed throughout her life. She seems to have an innate ability to continue to find a way out of difficult situations. So, even during the times Sister was in Baylor, and for the years she was married and living in other places with Mr. Smith, and even after Connie herself was married, the National Hotel was there exerting its influence and molding their lives. Who would get away from his roots?

Sister idolized Connie, who could do no wrong. One of the chief reasons for their rapport was that Connie played the piano on all occasions. She learned to play "Napoleon's Last Charge", "Tiger Rag", and numerous World War I songs by simply listening to her mother play them. She would often sit on the floor with her ear up against the sounding board, listening.

Later in life, she played them without ever having seen the music. Jimmie's fantasy was for her oldest daughter to become a professional musician. She embodied all the dreams Jimmie had once had for herself. Connie had no teacher save her mother and in a few years, she was going to be ready for the concert stage. She was taught classical music from the outset; but what that girl could do for Jazz! We still love for her to play, for she can make a piano talk!

But alas for the "Best Laid Plans o' Mice and Men;" and also for those crazy mixed up glands. Connie reached maturity quickly. She was a leader in school, was always the center of a crowd and much in demand for music and dancing. But she decided she preferred life with Sylman Galloway when she fell in love with him while they were still Seniors in high school. They eloped all the way to Brother Wallace's house — where he united them in the holy bonds of matrimony.

Consequently, Sister crammed her dreams into her pocket and set about washing diapers and helping feed hungry children. They all lived together in the little house by the stand-pipe. Although Sylman was very smart, he had no training for good jobs; besides it was depression times, and none were available. So for several years Jimmie had to run up bills to feed and clothe the children; and she never got out of the habit. Even for years after Connie and Sylman had moved their little family to Skidmore where Sylman had secured a job with his brother, she was still paying out those bills at $5.00 per month. She saved dimes to buy the material for graduation dresses for JoAn and Sylvia and Jeannie even after they had moved to Webster. Her salary at the telephone office was never more than a pittance, but it was supplemented somewhat with money for private music lessons — which were always her pleasure.

A real emergency occurred when Connie had to go to the hospital in Marlin for a serious operation. Sister and Mama kept the children, and it was quite a task. Sister kept the girls up at her home and let them come down, occasionally, to the hotel. Neither of them was accustomed to taking care of such a rambunctious bunch of children. But the care of the baby, Robert Sylman or Bobbie, was left to Mama. One day she was just sure that he had swallowed a penny because one disappeared from the table near his crib. (Too bad that he hasn't clutched all pennies as tightly ever since.) Jimmie and the other children were definitely put on the alert to look carefully for the penny through all his stools for several days afterwards. But, alas! it was never found. So Bobby may still have the penny somewhere in his sytem and the National Hotel may have exerted a stronger influence on his life than he realizes. Well, "a penny saved is a penny earned."

Mama wrote in a letter to her niece, Vance: "I took the dear little baby with fear and trembling. I asked God's guidance and I feel that he answered my prayers and directed me to the right food and care. Oh, when his Mother came home from the hospital, the baby looked wonderful. She hardly knew him."

JoAn was 5½, Syliva was 4½; Jeannie was 2½; and Bobby was just a baby, but Mammy and MomMom (the children's pet names) were a force in their lives. Jeannie says that MomMom's hair turned white overnight. The next morning she marched the three girls down to Porter McCoy's Barber Shop and had their hair cut off. It was simply too much trouble to care for. They looked like little boys, and Connie cried when she saw them.

Sylvia remembers the location of the family rooms, particularly the bathrooms. One of those early days Mama put her on the pot to do her business, but she did not come back to take her off quickly enough to suit Sylvia. Mammy, her great-grandmother, called out: "Sit still, honey. Mammy will be there in a minute", to which Sylvia responded: "Well come on, you old Jackass," Mama was so tickled that she leaned up against the door facing and laughted heartily. She regaled me with this story when I came home from school.

Sylvia also remembers the beautiful, wonderful, ravishing hats that Robert made for their dolls, hats made of cardboard covered with cloth. How they treasured these hats; and the lesson they taught the little girls was that if you want to make something bad enough, you can always find suitable material.

Mammy had taught them to "make do" with what they had.

JoAn and Jeannie have faint memories of the hotel. JoAn was fascinated to watch Mama put her hair up on white kid curlers at night. She knows that Mammy was always there—her very heartbeat the pulse of the National Hotel. The children were never allowed to go upstairs. That was forbidden territory. However, they could go up as far as the first landing and this was their favorite haunt in the house, rivaling even the stoop back of the kitchen where the kitchen help sat to snap beans. Once, JoAn had the inestimable privilege of going upstairs with me, Aunt Ruth, to clean up a room. Her eyes bugged out at the wonderland of a forbidden place to a child.

Once, when Connie and Sylman lived in Skidmore, Sister (after almost having a nervous breakdown) went to visit them. Life was not easy for the Galloways. They had a hard row to hoe. But, as always, Connie managed to manipulate conditions happily. They went to baseball games, on picnics, and fishing trips, as those things were Sylman's favorite recreations. The three adults, four children and Queenie, the dog, all piled in their little car and went on their joyous way. Connie and Sister had learned the lesson well from Mama to be content in "whatsoever state" they found themselves. Sister went back to Franklin with renewed vigor and strength.

So the National Hotel had much weight in the early lives of Connie's children but not the same hold that it had on their mother and Aunt Frances. Those two who were so alike and yet so different. They were sisters and they grew up under the same environment; one would have expected them to resemble each other more. Looking back from the pinnacle of more than sixty years, they seem more alike now; yet in reality, they are not. Life does strange things to people in its changes and developments. They do not always turn out the way they seem headed as children, but are made over by strange patterns. Yet life goes on, and as they were in childhood, so they are in adulthood (molded and changed however by life's fortunes and misfortunes.)

Frances has a few scattering memories of her early life, of
Mama and of the hotel. One of her earliest recollections was of
Mama's little old tin bath tub, enameled inside and out and sitting up bravely on its spindly legs. Her first memory of living
was of her Mother in Mammy's car, old Studey, with its four little jump seats and its isinglass windows in the top which was
raised only when it rained. So her childish memories were of actual articles — and antique ones at that.

After supper in the summer, we would all sit out on the
front gallery of the hotel. Frances' lifelong interest in gardening
and antiques and beauty is demonstrated in her early interest in
things around the National Hotel, particularly the long
surrounding porch with bannisters — railings with posts in between — and big oak trees towering just beyond. There were
rows of rose bushes growing down the fence. Marshall Neil rose
bushes trailing up the back porch were covered most of the year
with beautiful golden roses.

All five of Mama's grandchildren inherited her love for
flowers. It was ingrained into them, although Robert is the only
one who followed horticulture professionally. Frances has
specialized in gardening and is never happier than when she is
working in her own or in Connie's garden. Connie runs her a
close second and has turned her special abilities to flower arrang-
ing. Minnie has lovely house plants and beautiful outside beds,
and Jean has the magic to make flowers grow.

Frances still remembers the ornamental iron fence around
the yard of the old hotel, the dozens of little lacy ferns, the
quaint old building with bay windows in front—all a part of her
childhood. They sat in these windows, playing their favorite in-
door game, Flinch. But Robert always cheated, and their game
ended with cards flying in the air.

When a new Baptist Church was being built, they had Sunday School temporarily in Mitchell Brothers' Bank Building.
The children had gotten the habit of going there every Sunday

morning. One Sunday, long after the congregation had moved to the new church building, Connie and Frances did not come home after Sunday School. The entire family went all over town looking for them. Morgan finally found them about mid-afternoon sitting on the steps of the Mitchell building. Frances looked up tearfully and said plaintively, "Connie and me came to Sunday School, but nobody else ever did come." Frances felt that if she could ever say after some misdeed, "Connie did it, too," that things were O.K.

All the children were crazy about their Aunt Ruth. They hated for me to go away to college, and it was a red letter day when I'd come home with my choice presents for them. I was just enough older that they all respected me and loved me dearly. Witness the three pictures of me in antique frames on the walls of Frances' lovely new house in Houston. Through the years I have always been welcome at any of their homes, and my apartment is full of mementoes which they have brought me from everywhere. The children's love for me has been one of the features of my life for which I have been the most grateful. They have enriched my life and have made me very happy.

Robert and Minnie had the measles when they were children. They had to stay in a darkened room and were not able to use their eyes. Mama told Frances to sit with them and to read them anything they wanted. Robert was an inveterate tyrant and he made her read every word of the Dave Fearless series — to which Minnie listened also, but except for taking up the time, it is doubtful that she enjoyed Dave's adventures any more than Frances did. Frances wished that she'd have the measles too and the mumps and whooping cough. She envied their special privileges when Minnie and Robert were sick. But she never did have the diseases and neither did her Aunt Ruth. The only time Frances ever remembers being sick was when she was all of four years old. She got to sleep in her mother's bed, and Morgan brought her in "mater soup" and oranges. Oh, being sick brought its own rewards!

Not often did the child see a doctor. Once Dr. Curry was called for her, and she was enthralled when he took out his gold watch to count her pulse. I don't know who came the nearer to fainting — Mama or Frances — when Dr. Curry blew his nose on her sheet. Probably Frances because she had always been clean to a fault and she has a proclivity for fainting. She fainted dead away when she was vaccinated; she lost consciousness at the picture show seeing the adventures of Clara Bow; and she fainted several times while she was in nurses' training. During World War I, Aunt Ruth and her best friend, Mildred Beall, would sing "The Yanks Are Coming, The Yanks Are Coming." Frances would be terrified. She had no idea who The Yanks were nor when the confrontation would take place; but when the singers would get to "The drums rum-tum-ing everywhere", Frances would shrink in horror and hide under the bed.

When she was a child, Frances usually had a solution to every problem. Once after Mama and the three Rucker children had returned from Gainesville, there seemed no solution to their perplexities. The children fussed and fought all the time. Usually Connie and Frances teamed up and Minnie and Robert were allied; I served as moderator. Finally, Frances came up with the ultimate solution: "Mammy, you put your children in the back 'ard and Mama can put her children in the front 'ard." She really needed an explanation, though, the time the squirrel bit firmly into Minnie's finger while it was being transferred from box to cage. It's a thousand wonders that she didn't have rabies.

When they lived in Marshall, Sister worked and went to school. Frances often swung in a peach tree while waiting for her mother to come home. She loved the sweetgum and persimmon trees and ate of the fruit of the black walnut tree. She and Connie often sang little duets, in particular one that Mama had taught them at the National Hotel.

"Oh, Lord, don't you remember Daniel in the Lions' den?
Remember, Jonah, in the belly of the whale and then,
The Hebrew children from the fiery furnace,

82

So the Good Book do declare;
And Lordy, mercy, if you can't help me,
For goodness sake don't you help that bear.''

Miss Axtell stayed at the hotel all one summer with her nephew, Dick; she organized a class in china paining. Frances was more than thrilled to be allowed in her class. That was her first attempt at painting and she loved it. For more than a decade, Frances gave most of her spare time to painting. It was artistic — a natural for her. If she had devoted her full energies to painting, she might have become a real artist. But when she gave it up, she no longer had any interest in it whatsoever, and turned to other pursuits.

Frances loved intensely as a child; she did not love widely. She did not have the genial "I love everyone" attitude that Connie had. She "loved not wisely but too well," as the poet put it. She had a passion for small things, particularly small animals. Once a jolly, carefree group of young men came to the hotel and stayed for a week advertising Calumet Baking Powder. These boys had three dogs — a big one that was called "Calumet" and two little puppies named "Sooner" and "Later." It was love at first sight on Frances' part. They were the idols of her eye and she played with them incessantly. But Fate willed other than perpetual happiness for them. One day little Sooner was run over in the street by a passing car and was killed. Frances was inconsolable. She cried her heart out and then disappeared. The entire family searched for her for hours. Finally, they found her fast asleep under her mother's bed where she had crawled away to lick her wounds.

Connie and Frances had both always loved their Uncle Bob. He was a hero to them and they loved anything he gave them. Once he brought in a little pig to Mammy to eat up the hotel slop. This little pig became Frances' especial care, and she spent long hours leaning over his fence and whispering sweet nothings to the little piggy. By fall, he had become a big hog and was ready to be slaughtered. You can imagine the consternation in Frances' soul and the disturbance she raised when he was brought in — roasted — on a big platter with a beatific expression on his face and a round, red apple in his mouth.

When they lived in Wheelock, Frances had two pet chickens and a hound dog which she called "Hound Pup." The chickens liked to sleep in trees, and the child often had the whole family up at night chasing them down and out of her tree house. They, too, soon met the common fate of other feathered friends in the soup pot. She only got to keep Hound Pup a short while for he, too, was killed.

It seemed to Frances that everything bad happened to her. She was almost afraid to love anyone or anything for fear something bad would happen to it. She could not accept the truth that everyone else had troubles also, the fact that the vicissitudes of life happen to all of us. No! Troubles have always loomed larger in her own life, and she talked about them so that she almost made others agree with her. It is as if an ominous cloud is hovering over her and her frequent cry is "Why do these things happen to me?" It is hard for her to realize the plain and sober truth that Longfellow expressed:

"Thy fate is the common fate of all,
Into each life some rain must fall,
Some days must be dark and dreary."

It seems that Frances had lived not one but four lives: a child, a nurse, a married woman and now, a life alone. Each existence has been dominated by her desire to help others, to be of some use to the world. Albeit her world.

After graduation from high school, Frances chose nursing as her vocation, and took her training at the Central Texas Baptist Sanitarium in Waco, Texas. This pleased Mama very much. That night her tongue was loose at both ends. Some of the things I remember that she told me were: "Oh, Ruthie, I cannot tell you how happy I am that Frances has chosen to be a nurse. That is what I have always wanted to be, and I had hoped that one of my daughters would choose the nursing profession."

I replied, "Mama, you hurt my feelings. I could not have been a nurse. The very idea is abhorent."

"No, dear, I did not mean that I was hurt because you nor Jimmie wanted to be a nurse. But this is the happiest day of my life. I feel that Frances is mine, too, and that my life will now be complete. You know my mother, Sara, was a natural born nurse. She was always ready at the borning or the sickness or the dying of anyone in her community. She would take her little leather pouch containing her Indian knowledge of herbs and simple medications plus her innate desire to be of service to humanity, and she was a welcome visitor in any home where there was sickness."

"Mama, dear, I know you are a fine nurse because you always cared for all of us. I think you know more than most doctors know about doctoring." (How true my words turned out to be when sixty-five years later my daughter Jean and I still use many of her simple remedies. And we take the words of her little white medical dictionary as the law and the gospel.) Mama wrote in a letter to her niece, Vance: "Frances has chosen for her life's work the nursing profession. Who can tell where all their lives will lead? I can only hope that each one will honor God in his daily life and be of service to others in the hunger of our hearts." Frances specialized in obstetrics because (so she said) a new baby was God's greatest gift to the world. She was never to have a child of her own, but she was to be foster mother to hundreds of newborn children — most of whom made their mothers very happy.

One day while she was in training, she asked Dr. Dudgeon if he remembered the operation he had performed on her Uncle Bob in Franklin. He replied: "Do I remember it? That was the event of a lifetime. My operating table was the dining table set up on the back porch with a sheet spread over it. The natives were gathered all around — even up in the trees. I'll never forget when I cut into that man's abdomen; the corruption and bruised blood gushed as high as the ceiling."

A few years later, Frances came to Tyler to be head of obstetrics in the new Mother Frances Hospital. She arrived in the East Texas city a few days early in order to visit with Mama and me. The formal opening of the hospital was not to be until the following week, but it had a premature baptism of blood; its doors were opened to the victims of the New London school disaster. The call went out over the radio for all available doctors and nurses; a friend drove her to New London immediately where she made some semblance of order out of the chaos as she laid out row after row of little bodies in a vacant store building.

After Frances met and loved and married Doyle, he did not want her to work outside their home, so she turned her passions to keeping house and gardening — often working too hard to suit her husband. But she paid up her nurses' dues each year so that she could turn back to her former love if the occasion demanded. Throughout her married life she strove to be a good wife and to make her home as beautiful and well cared for as possible. She loved Doyle deeply and spoiled him unmercifully. He was a wonderful son to Jimmie, a kind grandson to Mama, a true brother to Connie, and a real pal to me.

I always felt very close to Frances and Doyle. Lem loved them. They stood up with us when we got married, and were later made Jean's god-parents. Frances came to me in Los Angeles after my daughter was born and she has come again and again, even to taking me in the city traffic to the opthamologist and the hospital this year when I had eye surgery. Playing bridge has been her consolation. She is a real master. Also, she can sew more beautifully than anyone I know.

During the last few years of Jimmie's life, Frances devoted her entire ability and energy to her mother. She went to the Nursing Home every day to care for her loved one when neither she nor Connie could look after her any longer in their own houses. Jimmie was the prettiest, the cleanest, the best cared for patient there. Frances and Connie cared for her patiently and gladly.

Frances has never gotten over the loss of her mother; and when that loss was followed a few years later by Doyle's death, she wanted to crawl away somewhere for consolation. She felt that her dark cloud had descended. My niece finds her main solace in her devotion to her family, in her bestowal of favors to them, and in trying to make her home as beautiful and well kept as possible.

Frances is a perfectionist. She demands that quality of herself and expects it of others — often to her sorrow! She thinks of Mammy frequently and of how she had to start all over. Frances has the example set before her of tireless work for that which she wants to accomplish, the chief difference being that Frances is almost forty years older than Mama was at her husband's death and that problems become more difficult for all of us as time goes on.

She is indeed a very private person. It is hard for her to open up to people. Whereas her mother knew everyone in Franklin, Frances can count on the fingers of one hand the houses she was ever in back in the old hometown. She had close friends among the boys and girls, but the depth and the warmth of her nature have seldom been shared with others. However, she is very interested in people in her early life. She has many memories of things and of people there; witness the roll of old-time members of the Franklin Baptist Church. Witness, also, her deep interest in the high school graduates of 1925 which group I spoke to last year. She spent a night in a motel in Hearne reading aloud every name in the Franklin phone book and recalling many things about the people in Franklin, and her marvelous memory makes them come alive! She treasures most the memories of her family and of the National Hotel. Deep down, Frances is strongly fastened to her roots. She keeps these tokens among her souvenirs.

Life has taught Frances tolerance. She makes more allowances now, for others' foibles. She takes advice from Connie and from others in her family when making decisions; she tries to comprehend that "No problem" is a good phrase in its way. As she said recently: "Each person has to live his own life and he should do the things he loves to do best. We are all different. We are all individuals."

MINNIE AND ROBERT

The Wizard of Loveliness—With Emphasis on Minnie Abbey Rucker Cole, Called Minnie.

Minnie was a very little girl and Robert was a baby when brother brought them home to Mama and me after the death of their mother, Ruth. Mama accepted them gladly and raised them as if they were her own. They were just the same as my younger brother and sister — even to their last name. Many of the drummers who came to the Hotel regularly thought we were of the same family. None of us ever knew the difference. They are my younger brother and sister.

Brother had a soft spot in his heart for Minnie. His nickname for her was "Kooter", and he was proud of her. He called Robert "Buddy" or "Bud" or "Little Pig." The nickname "Buddy" stuck and to some of his old-time friends he is still "Buddy Rucker." But he grew very tired of it and proposed to Mama that he would henceforth call her "Mother" instead of "Mammy." In return, he was to be called "Robert," his real name. The rest of us followed her lead, as we did in so many things, and also called him "Robert" — sometimes "Bob." But his sister was called "Little Minnie" all of her young life. You may guess who was called "Big Minnie" or just "Minnie."

It took a while for the two little children to get accustomed to living at the Hotel. Minnie followed Mama around, pulled on her coat tails and begged, "Granny Rucker, soup Minnie." But she soon shortened this to "Mammy" as she became more vocal. They played with old Sport, their big collie dog, in the swing in the back yard. When their pet died at the age of fifteen, Minnie delivered herself of this oration at his funeral: "Old Sport was given to me when I was a baby, and he was my shadow. He went to school with me every day and then he'd turn around and come home. He was a most intelligent dog. Sport would never bark nor growl at a drummer; but just let anyone else come in this yard and he'd come unglued."

The four played together very well. Frances had been given a squirrel in a little box. All the children worked all day on a cage for it, putting into it every bit of wire and screen they could find. There arrived the moment of its transfer from the box to the cage. Frances told of the event: "As usual the hardest task was put off on me. Well, I reached into the box and grabbed it by the tail. It swing wildly and widely in the air as it tried to get away. In midair it connected with Minnie's finger and clamped hard with its teeth. Minnie bears the scars to this day." They all screamed wildly. Morgan came running and literally pried his jaws open, muttering Polish all the time. It's a thousand wonders the child didn't have hydrophobia.

Minnie grew up working in the hotel. She would go up the street with money clenched tight in her little fist and buy things for the Hotel—even before she started to school. Once she went up to Cousin Jim's store and bought a dozen pair of shiny rayon socks, tearfully explaining to Mama: "They didn't cost anything. Imogene just charged 'em." Mama made her return them, but let her keep three pair. Mama went off mumbling, "That Minnie! Born with a silver spoon in her mouth." Mama had a wide reputation for the good food served in the hotel, and people would drive for miles and miles just to eat there. As Minnie grew up, she planned the menus and bought the food. She often went to the grocery store in the morning and selected the vegetables to be served at lunch, leaving a list for the ten o'clock delivery. She bought all of Mama's clothes, ran up the back way to Mr. Scott's market for special cuts, did all the banking business.

Minnie Cole still has the knack of planning good meals and preparing them easily; that ability never was mine. I also could buy food and plan menus, but working with food never came easy to me. I suppose Mama didn't need me to help as much when I was little. She was older with Minnie and had to leave more of the actual work to her; I could have been found "sucking" a book, as Mama called it, or reading and memorizing poetry or trying my hand at writing. Minnie usually baked four cakes every Saturday to serve with home canned peaches or pears which Mama had put up. Mama paid her twenty-five cents a cake. She learned early to stretch her money and it has paid off, just as cooking skills have stood her in good stead.

Even though we always had a maid, any of the family could do things upstairs in a pinch. If someone checked out late, or if a room were needed, as often as not, Minnie went upstairs and cleaned up the room in a jiffy. In fact, she was as efficient in the hotel as she was in school and later as a teacher, worker, wife and mother. She went quietly and competently about every task, and the result was perfect.

Minnie started to school at age five and one-half. She had played dominoes, made change, and shopped for the hotel; so school work presented no problem. She was precocious and always made straight A's. Once when she came home and bragged about making an A in something difficult, Mama muttered: "Humph! That's no more than I expected."

In fact, she went to school for the first month reading a book propped behind her school book, a book that her teacher, Mrs. Cole (the same first grade teacher who had started us all in school), had told her not to take home. I knew that Minnie considered the spanking given her on her legs a permanent disgrace because I, too, had once received such punishment. When Mama lived in Austin Minnie was in the sixth grade; she had learned all about fractions in just two months after returning to Franklin. In high school, her favorite was Miss Johnnie and she loved everything the lady taught, including history and Latin. She loved all extracurricular activities, particularly debate. Once they went to A&M for a tournament, and Mr. Wilcox (who had stayed at the National Hotel frequently when Minnie was a little girl) was one of her judges; he remarked: "My goodness! Don't tell me that intelligent young woman is the little girl at the Hotel." As Morgan said, "I tell you when they made that Minnie, they lost the pattern." Yes, it was no wonder that Mama wasn't surprised when her granddaughter was graduated from high school as valedictorian.

Minnie was like me in many ways. There was no doubt about our love for each other and about our mutual admiration for each other's individual accomplishments; but she, after all, was quite different from me.

In the first place, she, somehow, got by with so many things that I never could. Perhaps Mama was just older, but her attitude toward Minnie was quite different from the attitude that she had had and was always to have toward me. She had mellowed somewhat and Minnie was permitted to do many things that I had never done. She wore rouge and lipstick and high heels earlier; Mama let her date younger; Minnie usually had her own way; she could wind Mama around her little finger. She never lied to Mama; she didn't have to. If Minnie did it, it was all right.

She told me how she got her own way with Mama. "Oh, it's pretty easy, Aunt Ruth. Mammy just can't stand for me to be left out of things. So I told her a sad tale about everyone in my crowd going to the skating rink except me. I made her think they didn't ask me because they knew she wouldn't let me go. This made her quite angry, and even though she hates skating rinks with a purple passion, she said I could go."

Minnie had ready-made dresses earlier than I did. She did not like the homemade ones (as I had not), so she was allowed to buy them. She went to work for cousin Jim Truett in his dry goods store. She also worked for Mr. Elmo Reynolds on Saturdays and was allowed to spend her money as she wished; and you can bet that the majority of it was spent on clothes, make-up, and accessories for herself. As a consequence, she developed early a sense of style and of the value of a dollar, which is still true today.

Even as a child, she had been very particular about her clothes. She did not like to wear the same dress twice in a row. Mama always sorted her dresses in a separate stack, and Minnie had to iron them herself. Morgan would often iron them specially for her saying: "You just leave your dirty things here, honey, and I'll slip in later and wash them out for you."

At the end of the season, Mr. Elmo would give Minnie all sorts of things: novelty tennis shoes, hosiery, purses, shoes, cosmetics, jewelry, pens, pencils, stationery, house shoes. Oh! Her possessions were legion. But Mama made her throw away an all-rubber bathing suit he gave her. Mama was adamant about it, exclaiming: "Why, Minnie Abbey Rucker. I'll never in the world let you wear a disgraceful thing like that. I'm surprised that Mr. Elmo gave it to you."

A U.S. Rubber Co. representative gave her the first pair of Keds that were ever in Franklin. He told her: "Why, Miss Minnie, that will be the best advertisement I could have. You have such pretty little feet."

"I always felt that there was an unusual tie between Minnie and me," Frances said. There was only two weeks difference in our ages, and we have always been in the same room at school. I loved to go out to the Barnes' with Minnie. I felt that they were my relatives too. I would go with Aunt Mady in her little buggy. A small box in the back was my special seat. But I'll tell you something that I did not like — sleeping with Minnie. She always wanted to sleep right under you."

One of Minnie's favorite stories about Mama was the one about Mattie Frances Pierce, a girl who brought milk and butter to the hotel for sale. Invariably, she would ask in her whiney voice, "Whatcha doin Miz Rucker? Sweepin?" or "cookin", or "servin" or "ironin", or whatever Mama was doing at that point in time. Finally, in desperation, Mama answered, "No, Mattie Frances, I'm parching peanuts."

Robert was the bane of Minnie's existence. He slept on a folding bed in the hall outside his sister's door and tormented her unmercifully. Once when a girl was spending the night with Minnie, he rigged up a ghost to scare them. He took the breast bone of a turkey and tied a string on it so that it could be pulled up and down seeming to fly through the air. The resultant screams of fright were enough to satisfy him.

One summer, a seismograph crew was staying at the hotel. A young man about 21 took a special liking to Minnie, age 14. Mama would not let them go out of the house, so they played dominoes interminably. Finally, on Saturday night (the one night picture show), she did allow them to walk up the street to the show. Later, she sent Robert to the movie with special instructions to watch them and see that they did not hold hands. That was the night that Robert fell asleep on the front row. No one saw him, and Tally Grant, the cinema owner, locked up the show and went home. When Minnie and the young man got home, Mama asked: "Where is Robert? Oh, the poor little fellow must be asleep in that building, and it is locked up." So she telephoned Tally Grant, who had to come down to unlock the building. You may be sure that he shook Robert soundly to awaken him. Minnie and her date had to drag him home.

One night, Mama allowed Brother to take Robert and Minnie out to his cousin John Maddox's home to spend the night on the Navasot. The kids came back the next morning with wild tales. Robert, wide-eyed, told a real one: "Mammy, five of us kids slept in one bed together; and one of them wet on me."

Minnie added, "And, Mammy, there were bugs running up and down the iron bed posts."

Mama retorted: "I'm so glad you're here. I've been frantic — My God! Bed bugs!" She quickly stripped the children and put their clothes under the pot in the backyard to burn. Then she put Lysol in the bathtub and scrubbed them both, muttering in the meantime, "It's my fault. I ought to know better than to let your daddy take you off on some wild goose chase."

All summer long, Minnie had to withstand the boredom of Franklin. One got tired of playing dominoes and Flinch; certainly croquet was no fun with Robert because he cheated; O.K., she could play *The Stein Song* with Rudy Valley on their old record player. There was no radio or T.V. Nothing to do at night but get into mischief, read, or study. I guess one could sit in the porch swing outside Minnie's room and sing "Who, stole my heart away?" Ah, how well she remembered the first talking movie she ever attended, Al Jolson in *The Singing Fool.* That revolutionized going to the movies and Mama often took the whole family. We grew up with a real love for entertainment, fostered by Mama. How we all enjoyed the next few decades of movies — until today's "little screen" movies have captured our hearts. Only wait long enough and everything comes to T.V!

One Sunday afternoon, two boys from Bryan drove down the streets of Franklin. Minnie was sitting on the front porch of the hotel. As the boys passed by, they tipped their hats. After a few minutes, Martha Steele phoned to ask if Minnie would like to double date with Stuart Cole from Bryan. Minnie, of course, had to ask Mama's permission. I chimed in with: "Oh, Mama, let her go. It's just a Sunday afternoon ride." Mama finally consented, but added: "But don't you go joy riding all over the country, young lady. You'd better find you a good old boy from Booger County to go with."

This began several years of pleasant dating for Minnie. Stuart was a natural mechanic. He had made an attractive little sports car from parts of wrecked or discarded Studebakers, Fords, and Chevrolets. He called it his "Stuforlay" and it brought much happiness into their lives.

During the '30s, public dances were often held in the old Deckerd Bros. Furniture Store. Many one-night stands were played by leading bands of the day: Wayne King, Henry Busse, Glen Miller and even the incomparable Lawrence Welk. Stuart asked Minnie to go, and Mama acquiesced but delivered her usual words of wisdom: "Now, you stay in there on that dance floor It's when you get out in cars that trouble happens." I came over from Calvert with some friends; it was amusing to be going to a social affair with my little niece.

But Robert was the real star of that occasion. He witnessed the dance from the outside, climbed up and looked in at the window. Then, for days afterward, he gave a fashion commentary on the ladies' dresses. He didn't miss a detail of style, color, or ornamentation.

Stuart got Minnie a place to stay in Bryan with his Aunt Peg and Uncle Elon when she was invited to go to the A&M Ross Volunteers dance with the captain of the band. Minnie described the occasion thus: "That was one of the most memorable events in my life. The cafeteria was decorated like fairyland. And were those R.V.'s ever good looking. I think I sort of looked good myself in my heavenly blue, bugle-beaded, first real party dress, which Robert had bought for me. It cost all of $16.95. And to think it was ready-made!"

Through her years in Baylor College in Belton and teaching in Mumford, Minnie demonstrated her usual mental alertness and good judgment.

This reminds me of what Frances said about Robert lately. "He never seemed funny to us girls. We were so exasperated with him. And I don't see how Minnie could have ever been nice to him; he was such a pest. But I remember when everyone in Franklin saw him in that minstrel and thought he was hilarious. I must admit he was the funniest thing in the show. I am still convulsed when I think of him sitting there in his Mother Hubbard eating the big box of corn flakes, and gesturing with his cook spoon."

But actually, Robert got much more tolerable as he got older. I remember how beautifully he decorated the Baptist Church for Minnie's wedding to Stuart. It was a veritable garden spot with his handmade picket fences covered with vines from the woods, and everywhere there were baskets of lovely home-grown flowers. Years later, Robert was to decorate elaborate surroundings for impressive weddings, but never was there one more beautiful than his sisters'. The wedding was complete to the last detail — even to the crisp rustling of Mrs. Collier's silk petticoat. Mama was very proud of Minnie and proud of Robert's decorations. She felt that in Stuart, she had a new son who would care for Minnie always. Stuart's Bryan family and friends were conscious that they had acquired a priceless new member of the Cole family.

As indeed she has always been, she proved a real daughter to Mr. and Mrs. Cole and she has been more than loyal to all of Stuart's family and friends. Since Mama's death, we have always considered Minnie's home to be the half-way house for our family. Minnie has been a real sister to Robert. She helped him financially when he was a student, and she has been very close to him and Freda and their family through the years.

Minnie was a very loyal and wonderful daughter to Mama. She has been like another mother to my daughter, Jean. As a mother, she has gone all out and she has been amply repaid by the accomplishments of her daughter, Charlotte. I am so glad that Mama got to live a few years of Charlotte's life because she adored her. Lem teasingly remarked: "I tell you, honey, those Coles are really slow. Why they have been married for years, but the Lemmings had to give them the idea. And to think that their daughter Charlotte was born just nine months after our own precious Jean!" I'm so glad that Jean and Charlotte were so near the same age, since her first cousins are old enough to be her aunts and uncles.

Minnie has always had an unusual capacity for making and keeping friends. Through her work, her clubs, her church, her daughter and Stuart's family, she is a friend to practically everyone in Bryan. And she keeps their friendship with the same easy sense of informality, graciousness, unselfishness, hospitableness, and competence with which she prepares a meal in her own house, executes a responsibility, or gets up a program. I think that Mama would have continued to be proud of her namesake — Minnie.

The Wizard of Flowers — With Emphasis on Robert Henry Rucker Called Robert or Bob.

A towheaded, lonesome-looking little boy was Robert. To use a flower metaphor—and what could be more suitable for his life — he might have been called a "thorn among the roses". But with his own individual sense of humor, he would have called himself a "rose among the thorns". He played happily around the hotel in his small handmade shirts and pants; even the little suits he wore to Sunday School were handmade by Mama from old suits of brothers'. He was always accompanied by one or more females—a sister, a cousin, an aunt, or a grandmother. So he grew up feeling dissimilar to other little boys in town, feeling at odds also from the women in his family. He felt that he was an outcast. He felt different. But he was the only one in his group with a penis and that gave him a nice distinction.

There were certain chores that Robert inherited by reason of his being a boy. He was always the bellhop and carried the guests' suitcases. Mama would call out: "Robert, you bring in the wood for the cookstove and the heating stoves. It's too hard a job for your Aunt Ruth and the girls." However, he was a natural comedian and would stand up on the woodpile and entertain the passersby. Mama would have to give him a "knot on the head" to get him to bring in the wood. When he was supposed to be out hoeing in the garden, he would stop everyone who came by for a conversation. Mama yelled to him from the back door, "Robert, quit sucking that hoe handle and get to work on those weeds."

Robert was always furious that the girls wouldn't let him play dolls with them, so he made up dolls of his own. One day the ice pick was his doll. He decided that his doll would go over and play with Connie's doll outside under the big trees, so he went walking it along "pick, pick, pick" over the ground. Suddenly Connie's scream of terror told him that the icepick had gone into her foot. You may be sure that sister did not wait for Mama to punish him.

Mama became completely exasperated with him and his dawdling so she went into a regular tirade. "I tell you, Robert, you are exactly like your grandfather. It would take Henry Rucker longer to get anything done than anyone else I ever saw but you. Your name should be Henry Rucker!" Robert looked at her in childish bewilderment and questioned haltingly; "Mammy, did you love him?"

Robert was always the one who was sacrificed in their play. Since he was in the minority, the girls all tormented him even though he addressed notes to them as "The Three Fairies". One day Mama had gone to town and returned unexpectedly. The girls had discovered that a bird had made a nest in the gutter around the long back porch of the hotel. There she had laid her eggs and hatched her baby birds. Their cheeping intrigued the four children so they found a rope, tied it around Robert's body, and lowered him over the back bannister. He would have had the birds in a minute more. Just at that second they heard

Mama's voice, ran to hide, and left Robert dangling there at the end of the rope. Mama was horrified at the sight. She rushed up the stairs and out to the back porch and pulled Robert up to safety by the piece of rope. "Mammy," he sobbed. "I thought I could reach the baby birds; but I couldn't. So I just held on tight to the bannister." Thus he escaped what could have been a nasty fall, but he did not escape punishment. Mama gave him a bad whipping. And the three girls, who had hidden in various places, escaped with only tongue lashings. Poor kid! He never even had a room of his own until the girls all went away from home.

Every fall Mama would load up the whole family in old Studey and take us to Waco for a day at the Cotton Palace. When Robert was four years old, we took this annual outing. After a long and tiring day, we were on the way home long after midnight; Mama was driving and Sister was sitting beside her — talking to keep her awake. The four children and I were in the back — all of us in various stages of sleep. We had driven through Marlin, Bremond, Hearne; from my place on the back seat I heard Mama and Sister talking about the towns and the route. Robert had been sound asleep in the bottom of the car on top of one of the folding jump seats. Finally, Mama said to Sister: "I can see the lights of Franklin."

Robert sat straight up and uttered one word which no one in the family had any idea he even knew and he promptly fell asleep again on the floor and had to be carried in when they reached home. The word was "Hallelujah!"

Robert was a very argumentative child. In fact, you might say he was contentious. When he would get into a dispute with Mama, she would say, "I'll declare, Robert, you can out-argue a government mule." Now, Robert didn't know nor care what a government mule was. He vaguely thought it must be something in Washington.

If he ever dared to contradict Mama she would threaten him: "If you don't stop that I'll beat you so hard you'll want to chew millet." Robert thought it was one word "chewmillet" until he was grown. Yet Mama wouldn't let anyone else touch him. He was her little boy.

She often talked to me about the children. "I don't know why the Lord has given them all four to me to raise. They are so different; I must remember that and deal with them in individual ways. I can make of them great men and women if only I can find the way to guide them aright."

A. U. S. geodetics survey team stayed at the hotel once for two or three months. It took them all summer to build a pipeline. Mama put them in double rooms and gave them special rates, but she didn't seem to be able to fill them up at the table. One of their favorite foods was ham and red eye gravy served on rice. One day when Robert was waiting on the table, he balanced a huge platter of the food on a big tray and reached over to put it on the table; the gravy spilled and ran down a man's back — covered with a clean white shirt — down to the floor where it congealed in a few minutes. Robert just did not know what to say — not even a word; so he merely put the tray down and took out at the front door. Mama was looking through her little peephole in the swinging door to the kitchen to see if the men wanted anything else to eat and she witnessed the whole affair. Robert still considers himself lucky that he did not get a good licking as a result.

Three generations of the black Porch family, headed by Aunt Fannie and Uncle Otter, had washed and ironed for the hotel and for Mrs. Rucker's family. I have talked about them before. Aunt Fannie's granddaughter, Margaret Rose, a young woman about Robert's age, would wash and starch and iron his white suit and shirts in the summertime. Margaret Rose declared herself: "Foe God, Mr. Robert, you could not excape me if I was only single and you was only a Niggah."

Aunt Fannie lived with her daughter Josie out in the country. Mama would send Robert to take food out to her on Christmas afternoon. As he approached her tumble-down shack (but always scrupulously clean) he would call out, recognizing that she was blind, "Hi, Aunt Fannie. This is Robert bringing you some Christmas dinner."

"Foe God, boy; you're my honey chile. Makes me feel like I wuz back at the hotel wid Uncle Otter. You all go back an' tell Miss Minnie I thanks her very kindly for sendin' me this good food." Years later, long after Aunt Fannie's death, I went out to Josie's to try to run down Mama's old organ which she had given to Aunt Fannie years before. But it must have long since been used for firewood, since no one ever realizes the value of a thing until it is gone!

Mama loved things that grew. One of her favorite pursuits after supper was to get out the Hastings Seed Catalog from Atlanta, Georgia and study its well-worn pages. She called it "The Wish Book". Robert shared this love with her. Mammy would order him anything he wanted from the book. So Robert first learned about plants by buying the seed from pictures in a seed catalog. Thus he learned one plant from another and became knowlegeable about them.

He loved flowers and he became personal friends with all the old ladies in town. Miss Jessie Patterson, Miss Maggie Mitchell, Miss Kate Mitchell; these ladies may have been considered "The Royal Family" of Franklin by some people — but they were close friends of Roberts'. They had mutual interests. At the Patterson home there was a pit greenhouse and at the Mitchell house a part underground brick structure, sort of a conservatory. Robert revelled in these and built an underground one for himself in the back yard of the hotel.

Miss Maggie had married Mr. John Mitchell who went to live in the Patterson home. Miss Jessie became a music teacher. She had a little studio on the school grounds where sister and I both had studied music. Miss Jessie went for a drive every afternoon in the surrey with the fringe on top. Miss Kate worked in the bank. She was a tall, elegant, beautiful lady. But they all spoke the language of flowers and Robert was very fortunate to have their friendship.

He was always play acting. I have already told about the time Mama made him wear a dress to town for punishment; but it turned out that he had a ball instead. The Chamber of Commerce gave a play — an evening of entertainment — one year. Robert was a colored girl in the play. He was a show within himself, and when he powdered his face with an enormous puff it brought the house down. Robert was a big tease; he tormented the girls so much that it made them furious. They did not realize until years later how cute and talented and dear he really was.

Robert never had anyone to tell him about sex. He learned about it in the hotel — often in a sordid manner. One of the first exposures was when he carried out Mr. Lime's rubbers in his slop jar. They wouldn't flush down the septic tank, so Robert would take them out in the back and bury them.

Mr. Lime was a fascinating person. He had travelled all over the world and thrilled the children with his stories. Some nights he would put a nickel on the screen and call to Robert and Minnie to come out and listen to some tales. Mama would say quickly: "Don't go. He's drunk." The kids were in Holy Terror of him and of the mosquito netting canopy over his bed. A woman appeared from his past and was shacking up with him at the time of his death. She left with one of his suitcases packed full of his possessions.

Whenever the magazine girls came to town they had to unload tons and tons of luggage. Robert carried all their suitcases upstairs, but he was amply repaid because they gave him a $2.00 tip. Immediately all the boys in Franklin who were called "Hard Pecker Boys" started flocking down to the hotel. One night they raised so much hell that Mama put them out in the middle of the night. They were no match for my mother's denunciations. A transplanted young Houstonian engaged in the legal profession lived at the hotel. He was a very staid, quiet man who taught a Sunday School class on Sunday. His room was at the top of the steps, the room which had once been Mr. Silverman's, a single room with a single bed. Mama had made some latticework frame half doors which hooked outside the wooden doors. They were covered with muslin and served for ventilation in those pre-air-conditioning days. As Robert took the luggage of the girls upstairs, he could see this regular guest standing silhouetted in his doorway. He wore a night cap and scallop tailed nightshirt which hung on him like a Jack as he was well endowed. It was a magnificent sight. One of the girls shouted to him: "You long codded son of a bitch, get your ass back in that room." The man slammed the wooden door and didn't come out again till after they were gone.

Room No. 12 had a private bath. It was rented to an old bachelor. Later, when he got married Robert carried up buckets of hot water for the man to take a bath. He bathed in front of Robert, who could see that this boarder was well endowed too.

Once, a man died in the hotel. They embalmed his body there before shipping it. Robert watched. The mortician cut his arm with a scalpel and placed a thing on it to draw blood. Robert became sick and could not watch the whole process. Mama called to him: "Come on, Robert, and carry down these three big slop jars. Bury the stuff in them out behind the garden and wash out the slop jars with lye."

When they took the coffin to the depot, they called Alma Gant's husband, Fred, who drove the dray. It was a heavy wagon with metal wheels and was pulled by two enormous Percheron horses. They were high steppers and were a real novelty. The only other Percheron horses that I have ever seen in my life — and only on TV at that — are in the Old Milwaukee Beer advertisements publicizing Budweiser Beer.

The dray was also used to bring the drummers' big trunks of samples from the depot to the National Hotel. They would be put off the train at the depot docks, then loaded on the dray and brought across the street in great style to No. 17, the sample room, where they were unpacked. Their contents looked like fairyland to the kids peeking in at the windows. Sometimes the drummers would stay for a week — never locking a door nor a window. Oh things were safe at the National Hotel — about sixty five years ago!

Robert lived on at the hotel after the other three children were gone. His last year in high school, then two years after he had finished school, and then the years in A & M, Mama turned to him and their relationship grew much closer. He learned to

103

appreciate and love her more and she loved him in return.

Mama had long wanted to rebuild the old hotel. She had gone through several renovations, repainting and papering and changing of rooms, but the building was essentially the same as it was when she had first bought it. It was her utmost desire to build a new hotel and she dreamed of and planned for it for years. They were wonderful plans for a woman of her age and lack of practical experience. They showed her native intelligence and her vision and hope. Robert and Mama were alone much of the time and he shared her dreams.

Mama's ideas were much beyond her times. We were all familiar with her oft-expressed notions. "They knew nothing about air-conditioning in those days, so I had windows put in every possible place and kept them all wide open. The cooking for the hotel has to be done on a big iron stove fired with wood, resulting in very hot temperatures in the kitchen. I had my stove specially made with some modifications. It was the first of its kind in Franklin. I knew from years of experience in operating a hotel that you needed two ovens — a cooking and a warming oven; also that there had to be a certain amount of cooking space on the top of the stove. So I made sure that in the fire box of the oven there was plenty of room for hot water to supply the two public baths in the hotel.

"I tell you, Ruthie, it is my desire to build a fifty gallon tank in the kitchen so that I can have hot and cold running water in every room in the house. I'll have an auxiliary unit installed and when the cookstove cools down at night, I can fire it up with gas. We'll get rid of all those old bowls and pitchers (and to think that I have only one of them now — and it has a big crack in it). I tell you we'll have a real modern hotel in Franklin."

This was a wonderful accomplishment in the days when no place, except big city hotels, had hot and cold running water.

The kitchen was made convenient and serviceable. In front of the stove, the dishes could be served on one side of the six-foot table and Robert or anyone working could pick them up on the other side. When the dishes were washed in a double sink they were put up in a cupboard on the wall. The salads were served on a separate table. There were huge vents and exhaust fans over the stove.

In the dining room at the back were two rows of tables for six people each, and in the front there were two rows for four each. There was an inviolable rule that the tables had to be kept neat and clean at all times, and that the counter and stools in front of it had to be wiped and shiny. There was a passageway behind the counter with a door into the office at the far end. Double French glass doors led from the dining room into the office.

Originally there was a water cooler in the corner of the office which Mama required us to keep full and iced at all times, but one day there came in the mail *The Special Hotel Equipment Catalogue* from Chicago; and the day of the cooler was over. Mama pounced on it delightedly. "Look, Robert, here is the latest thing in ice chests. The water runs over the coils and there is a fresh supply of ice water at all times. I'll venture this will be very welcome to thirsty travelers." This was just another example of Mama's ingenuity in providing for the convenience and comfort of her guests.

Robert recalls: "During the day I frequently saw her jotting down ideas on the backs of envelopes. These she would transfer to paper at night long after everyone else was in bed. She worked with a cedar pencil on large pieces of butcher paper. It was white with a faint tinge of pink, sixty-six inches wide, and comparable in texture to drafting paper. I know because I had to get it for her at Cousin Jim's Dry Goods Store. It withstood the graphite of the pencil, so she had to lick it for every mark. She worked painstakingly on all the details. This draftsman used a foot ruler like the one I had in school because she knew the plans had to be drawn according to scale. I'll tell you she used space relationships like nobody's business."

About this time, Mr. and Mrs. Schoenberg, a nice quiet, wealthy couple from Muskegon, Michigan stopped overnight in Franklin on their way to their summer house in Port Isabel, Texas. They liked the food and the treatment in Franklin so they stayed a week. They would come back nearly every summer. Soon, a solid friendship developed. They felt that most of the people in Texas were not energetic enough and were "asleep at the switch". One thing led to another. Mama showed them the plans she had made for the hotel and they were impressed, for a woman—a widow who worked so hard—to make such excellent plans. So they loaned her the money to build a new hotel.

Mama and Robert and I sat down one night just before she sold out and moved to Tyler to talk over the "new hotel". Mama opened the conversation: "Well, the hotel was just what I wanted it to be—all the things I had planned and dreamed. I just can't see why I couldn't make a success of it."

Robert responded: "And the Schoenbergs were so wonderful to you. They let you have the money at such a low interest, and they have extended the loan several times. I know they trusted you to plan and to run the business."

I chimed in: "Mama, don't blame yourself. The time was out of joint. Who could foresee the stock market crash and the great depression. The bottom just fell out of things for thousands of Americans with more money and more 'know how' than you have."

"If it could have been built in ordinary times, I could have made a success of it. I have done so in the past."

"And the times are changing so fast," I added. "Modes of trade have revolutionized in the last two or three decades."

"Travel is so fast nowadays. Drummers can come to Franklin driving a panel truck over well paved highways", commented Robert. "They can show their wares and be on to Austin, or Waco, or Houston by sundown."

"They do not come to Franklin and stay several days," Mama agreed.

I reminded her, "And you must remember that you are nearly forty years older and that you do not have several families of children and grandchildren to give you help at the hotel. It's just too much for an old lady to tackle alone. There are too many fast food places along the road, and motels are easier."

"I guess the day of the small town hotel is over," Mama reconciled. "I have a chance to sell it, and I believe I'd better do it."

When I taught in Calvert, I had a chance to see conditions

at home more clearly; so I made up my mind that Robert was a boy and that I was not going to take on the responsibility of sending him to college. He could just make his own way in the world. But I could not stand for him to turn into the town bum, so I told him one day: "Come on, Robert, we are going down to A & M College and find you a job. You've got to go to school." So we went and made a fortunate contact with Dr. Hensel, the head of the Landscape Art Department.

Robert and I had been interviewing him about the possibility of Roberts' being in his department. It seemed that he and the boy struck a responsive chord with their mutual love for flowers and plants. Dr. Hensel had taken us over to show us the college greenhouse, and I was silently coveting it and its advantages for Robert. So far he had known the name of every plant the professor had shown us. They stopped in front of an exotic plant and Dr. Hensel explained; "It is the gift of a former student of mine, a most unusual variety from the Orient." Then he called its name.

Robert immediately replied: "I'm sorry to contradict you, sir; but I think you are wrong. I believe it is of an entirely different family."

I was suffering acutely. A mere slip of a boy, a country town high school graduate daring to dispute the word of a Ph.D., the head of a department in a large college. But there was nothing I could do.

The professor said, "Well, son. Let's just go over to the library and settle this once and for all."

So we went to the library, Dr. Hensel just waving to the head librarian and muttering: "These people are my guests." We went up to the shelves, pulled down a ponderous tome and looked it up; and Robert was right. The days and nights of studying books and pictures had paid off. Dr. Hensel turned to me and said: "We've got to get this kid down here. He knows more about plants than any of my Seniors know." And from that moment on, he was Robert's staunchest friend.

I could write reams about Robert in college, his very fortunate marriage to Freda Carter, his three wonderful children (Bill, Stuart, and Mary Virginia), his army life during World

War II, his losing of his right leg in Africa, his three and one-half decades of life after the war — but that's another book. It's called "Life with Oscar" and is being written by Robert, himself. Suffice it to say that Robert's international service to the Garden Clubs of America, his active membership in the American Society of Landscape Architects, his strong consideration of the environment, his honors from the American Horticulture Society, his sincere and loving enactment of his duties as a family man, his enthusiastic support and hard work for the various college and community activities he has been associated with, his active living of Christianity, his brave, personal disregard of pain, and — above all — his lifelong devotion to beauty — all these, I affirm, have reflected the influence of Mama and of the National Hotel of Franklin, Texas.

The Wizard of Mathematics — With Emphasis on Jean-Willette Lemming Called Jean.

Mama's youngest grandchild, Jean Lemming, was born long after the National Hotel had passed out of our family. The divergence in ages among Mrs. Minnie Rucker's children and grandchildren is nowhere so evident. Jean is much more the contemporary of her great-grandchildren than of her grandchildren. Why, then, is Jean included in this chapter?

Why she was peculiarly the child more exposed than any of her children or her grandchildren to Mama's influence. Jean appeared on the scene at a time in Mama's life that she had more leisure to think and to talk than she had ever had before. Since I have attempted to make it clear time after time that Mama's influence and the influence of the National Hotel were one and the same, therefore Jean has been under the influence of the Hotel — even though she has never entered its portals.

I came back to Texas with Jean-Willette when she was less than two years old — and what a strange two years it had been, a child with a sick mother most of the time, in bed the first seven months of her life. A sort of hovering between life and death

JEAN

109

there in Los Angeles. The child had been cared for by a sequence of cousin, paternal grandmother, great-aunt, father, friends, and hired help with their own rules and regulations to go by.

But there was never any doubt about love. Lem adored her; but he was a very firm parent, expecting much of a tiny baby! When he would dress her in her cutest clothes, which she had received largely as presents from her mother's Texas friends, and take her for an afternoon ride in her baby carriage, he attracted much admiring attention from passersby. And when he took her for the monthly visit to the pediatrician, the nurses would gather around agape at the Sergeant who could care so well for his little daughter.

I loved Jean dearly, of course, and whenever someone brought her to my bed I was very happy. But I was quite ill, and I endured her crying and her sweet baby noises in tearful silence because others had to care for her and I did not want to be any extra trouble.

The year we lived in Yakima, Washington had been the most normal of her two years. I was literally "on my feet" again and we lived happily with Lem's job in the radio station. Witness the normalcy of the pictures of her own little garden and the one of her romping with Daddy Lem on a blanket in the back yard. But even though I feel it is important to establish Jean's personality, it is Mama's influence that is chiefly vital at the moment.

Another reason for Jean's extraordinary telepathy with Mama is their likeness both temperamentally and physically. Despite the differences in environment and mores, I frequently will know in advance Jean's exact reactions to a situation because they are so much like Mama's. They were cut from the same mold; their resemblance is uncanny; I almost gasp sometimes because they look so much alike. Two peas in a pod didn't have a thing on Minnie and Jean.

One day Mama said to her niece, Alys, when they met at the trash burner in the back alley between their houses: "Tash, I can't tell you what a joy it is for me to be able to help Ruth with her little girl."

"Aunt Minnie, please tell me why on earth Ruth came home? I thought she and Lem were the two happiest people in the world."

"I'll have to confess to you that I don't know any more than you do. Ruth has not told me, and I don't think she ever will. I just want her to know that I am here and she can come home if she wants to."

"That's just like you, Aunt Minnie. You've been swell about the whole thing. About Ruth getting married and moving so far away, and about your coming back to Franklin to settle down."

"Well, Tash, I wanted to be understanding, and I thought the time might come when Ruth would need my help. This is a welcome task."

First Jean and I lived in Temple for a year. I had a good job in high school, and fortunate circumstances led to our having a very good home. Robert gave me his old car when the government presented amputee veterans with new ones. Charles Watson, our landlord, took care of it for me as well as taking care of Jean and acting "in loco parentis" for her. We were as happy as we could be, living there together with our lives so empty of our loved ones. Having our own things around us helped somewhat. I found a wonderful nursery home for Jean, and though she cried every time I took her, the lady who kept her said I was no sooner out of sight than she was playing happily. She was always glad when Mama came to visit us and she stayed contentedly with Mama in Franklin for two or three weeks at a time during my speech contest season or just before a play production.

Mama wrote me in a letter after she had made us a visit: "I haven't thought of a thing since I left there except my baby. Wish I had her all the time. Wish she could stay with me and go to school; it would be so much fun. I am sending her a little school bag which will keep her books and papers all nice and clean for years if she will take good care of it."

I think Jean almost welcomed these interludes with Mama

111

because it was nice to be a one-gal audience for Mama's tales, but she was glad enough to return home with me.

In Norman, Oklahoma, too, I was fortunate to find a woman with a nursery school who would keep her overnight whenever my boss would send me out of town. We were lucky to find a place for us to live which was very near Bob's flower shop because I worked there often when I was not at the Family Life Institute at the University of Oklahoma. We had the downstairs apartment in a duplex. I remember well the time one of my former students from Tyler came to see me and we sat in the swing on the front porch and talked for hours. Jean was not accustomed to my giving so much attention to anyone but her, and she gave vent to her emotions by taking a little sack of flour and pouring a steady stream of it around the walls, doors, windows, and every single piece of furniture. Of course her punishment was to clean up every bit of it. But I also had to work at it for several weeks. She would also cry whenever we would go to restaurants to eat with anybody and be very obstinate about her food. This was her own childish way of securing attention for herself and getting to be the center of interest. Sad to say this reminded me frequently of Mama.

Oh, she was pig-headed all right. Consider her actions the day of the bad snowstorm when no buses ran anywhere but the one to North Campus where our office was located. Even Marion Evans, our sweet secretary, did not come, and Jean literally could not get to nursery school; the roads were blocked. So — much to her delight — I bundled her up and took her with me, not planning to tell my boss since I was sure she would not like it. The minute we reached the office I telephoned Dr. Alice Sowers to tell her that I was there — albeit about two hours late. She was overjoyed and started giving me instructions for more work than could have been accomplished in four days.

The office was oppressively hot from the electric heater which had been left on all night, and Minnie (Jean that is,) wanted to be comfortable. So she started taking off her clothes, layer by layer, throwing each article in a different direction and clapping her hands and dancing in glee until she was stark naked. All the while, I was gesturing to her frantically to stop. I was in terror that someone would come in before I could complete the conversation with Dr. Alice. But our secret was well kept and no one ever knew that Jean spent the entire day with me at North Campus.

This makes me think of the day I walked out of the Laundrywell in Norman. Jean and I gathered up all our clothes one Sunday morning and went over to the nearby laundry to wash them. We had carried them inside and had them sorted out in appropriate tubs full. Then I went over to the man who ran the place, asking, "May I have change for a dollar, please?"

To which he replied: "Indeed you may, ma'am, and may I say that's a pretty little granddaughter you have there."

I turned and with the usual Minnie-like toss of my head and her dread of growing older, gathered up my clothes and stalked out to go to another laundry across town. Even though I could have been chronologically her grandmother, as my gray hair indicated, the fact remained that I wasn't; moreover, I did not intend to be reminded of it.

Later we moved back to Texas, to Wharton, where the only place that I could find to live was a big old two-story house on which the rent was so high that I had to sub lease rooms to make it. This was fortunate, though, because I had some help with Jean when I had the worst scare of my life. The doctors pronounced the dropsy disease she had as "Gillian Barre Syndrome." She had to stay off her feet entirely, and have complete bed rest. You can imagine how difficult this was with an active child like Jean — and with me in school all day. I would get up every morning at 5:30, prepare us a little breakfast, then wrap Jean in a blanket, carry her downstairs and go to the car, go out and get the nice practical nurse who cared for her, drive them back and carry her back upstairs — then, I'd be on my way to school by 8:00 o'clock. It must have been Mama's spartan-like temperament which carried us through this bleak experience. Of course, Mama would have come to Wharton in a minute, but she was no longer physically able to cope with a sick child in a strange house.

When we moved to the little home in Dr. Rugeley's back

113

yard, it was large enough for us on account of a little storeroom which he let us have in his backyard for Jean's playhouse. It was ideal. She had boxes made into dressers, her big dolls and her collection dolls, each one with a drawer for her clothes in my old Baylor College wardrobe trunk, little cookstove and utensils, mud pies, miniature furniture in doll houses — oh, all sorts of wonderful things. But one night a tragedy occurred. Some neighborhood vandals broke in and scattered and destroyed almost everything — including a box of Christmas tree decorations which had gone back to Lem's childhood. Only one ornament was left intact. Jean has it today, taped tightly in its container but never used for fear it will be broken. But she had to live without these things — surviving, enduring somehow even as Mama did.

The ability to spell was left out of Jean's makeup. She differed from Mama in this respect because Minnie could spell and give the meaning of practically every word in the dictionary. Although my daughter is a wizard at mathematics, she has difficulty spelling the word. When she was in girl scout camp near Conroe, she wrote asking me to send her "rido". I finally figured out that she wanted her "radio". Just last year she wrote on the blackboard a mathematics assignment that was due before "Chrismas". B.J. (before Jean) I had thought that good spelling was an indication of intelligence; however after a lifetime of trying, I have decided that there will always be secretaries and dictionaries for people with her brand of knowledge.

Mama's lifelong love of education has passed on to all of us. Jean never had a chance. It was a way of life and she was expected to get the best education possible. So she has done so. She was selected the best math student in Wharton High School. She was a member of Phi Theta Kappa in Wharton County Junior College. She took a B.A. degree in math from the University of Texas, and has an M.A. in math from Louisiana State University. She has had several postgraduate courses from the University of Houston. Now, she is teaching in Sam

114

Rayburn High School in Pasadena and in Houston Community College at night or on Saturdays.

There was never any doubt about her field. It became a commonplace truism that at the beginning of every school year, the teacher returning the first set of papers would ask: "Who is Jean Lemming?" After Jean had timidly identified herself the teacher would add: "This paper has all the information correct, but there are forty misspelled words"; or "Half the words are not spelled correctly"; or "The spelling is intolerable."

But this same child seldom brought home anything less than 100 on math. And she was a whiz at drawing stage sets for her mother's plays—just as Mammy used to draw hotel plans till far into the night. In math, Jean had no one to compete with. I think she chose this subject so she would not have to compete with me. There was no doubt about my lack of knowledge in this field, but I have encouraged Jean to do her best in what she felt she could excel in. She is very practical; she can cook and sew. I was determined for her to have these skills. She can do things with her hands. I always greet her with a list of things to do whenever she comes to my apartment. Again, in this respect she is much like Mama who, I felt, could do anything.

Jean grew more confident of my love for her. She was surer of her own place. I don't think she has ever been jealous enough to sprinkle flour on Paul, Mary Lou, LeRoy, Sylvia, Reda, Orion, Patsy, Ed, Mary Bea, Norma, David, Mary Frances, Wilda. They and myriads more have my especial love; Jean loves them too. They are my students. But there is only one Jean.

One of the funniest things that I remember happening transpired on Jean's baccalaureate Sunday. Rabbi Kahn of Houston was the speaker. He announced as his subject: *Don't Follow the Lemmings.* As soon as he made it known, he had lost that audience. There was a general wave of inattention, a craning of necks in Jean's direction, and a murmur which almost overpowered Rabbi Kahn's advice to be an individual and not to follow the crowd; a little more definition of the lemmings; and a description of them blindly following the leader into the sea. Later on when we introduced ourselves to him, he understood the inattentiveness of the audience. I think this quality of standing up for her own individuality — in other words, not being a lemming — was certainly fostered by her grandmother.

Somehow, Jean was a sad little girl. She was somewhat of a loner. She coveted the love of others, but she wended her way through the crowd mostly by herself. Oh, she was popular enough, but there was usually a pensive expression on her face, a sort of longing. For what? I cannot be sure. Perhaps a longing for the love of a father from whom she was separated by his own decision. Perhaps a longing for something that would make her mother smile again. Perhaps a longing for a normal home with two parents. Who knows? Or perhaps the expression was one of loneliness, a loneliness for that which she had once had and would never have again.

But there was one place where Jean knew she was first and where she was never lonesome — her Mammy's house. They spent many nights there completely alone because Jimmie worked at the telephone office. They would snuggle close together in the Jenny Lind bed in the back bedroom of the Hurley house and neither of them could have been happier. Mama would launch into some story about her childhood and Jean would listen — entranced. Many of them she had heard before, but one of the joys of childhood is to hear again and again one's favorite tales. Accounts of her half-Indian great-grandmother held the child spellbound. She could almost see her wearing her little black bonnet and carrying her little black satchel when she went to see the sick. Also, stories about the little black dog and their mutual love. And the tale of the night her Uncle Nat had come in after swimming the river. Jean could almost feel his clothes, frozen and standing upright. Oh the confidence those two shared!

And the wonderful things Mammy could do and could make! Why in the world hadn't she taught Mama Ruth to make things? The quilts and their designs, how to plant beans and tomatoes and cucumbers, and how to plow them. Jean's lifelong love of growing things was well established there. And the grape jelly and strawberry preserves Mammy could make; nothing like them could be bought in the stores. And most marvelous of all,

Mammy could take a real live chicken, wring its neck, and the chicken would flop around dying on the ground. What wonderful fried chicken it could turn into, just like those Mama bought in the grocery store, without Mammy's magic. Years later, Jean would think of some tale that Mammy had told her — but mostly they were absorbed into her childhood and became a real part of her personality — again, that old National Hotel influence!

It had always been a special privilege to sleep with Mammy. Connie had claimed that particular favor when she was a little girl. Minnie had considered Mammy her own individual property and she was jealous of Frances and Connie when they came to visit. But Jean was the most successful of all. When her mother would go away on a speech trip, there was no competition. The two of them would settle down together in the Jenny Lind bed, talking about old times to their heart's content.

One night Mammy launched into a long familiar tale. "I tell you, honey, that was the worst storm I have ever seen in my life. In just two more nights we would have been safe in the harbor of New York City. The captain of the ship said it was the worst storm he had ever experienced. Why we all got very sick, especially your Mama Ruth. She was just a little girl then, about like you."

"Mammy, dear, I can't imagine Mama being a little girl. Next you must please tell me about her being a little girl in the National Hotel. But now I want to hear about her being sick in New York."

"Oh, she was. She couldn't go out with Tash and me to see the sights of The Big Apple. We got the maid to stay with her at the hotel."

"She had a baby sitter?"

"They didn't call them baby sitters then, honey. But the maid was real nice and stayed with Ruth until Cousin Tash and I came in about 2:00 a.m. The next day, Ruth was able to go with us to see Grant's Tomb and the Statue of Liberty. Now it's too late to talk anymore tonight, honey. I'll have to tell you tomorrow about going on to West Virginia to see Aunt Jim and Connie."

"And to think Frances wasn't even born then." Jean loved these sessions!

The only other place where she was as happy was when she went to Bryan to stay with the Coles. Minnie was just like her mother and Charlotte was just like the often desired sister she had never had. They played happily for long hours with mud pies, going swimming in the nearby park, and twirling their batons. Food had never tasted so good as at Minnie's. Jean wondered why her mother could not cook like Mammy and Minnie could.

One of her favorite persons in Franklin was Mrs. Ben Love, whom we all called "Miss Gussie". She came by one Saturday to take Jean for a ride and she later reported her conversation to me.

"Are you going to Sunday School in the morning?" she had asked.

Jean replied, "Yes Ma'am, we're going. Mama used to be a member of this church."

"Do you understand what 'being a member' means?"

"Oh, yes, Mama has explained it to me."

"And what church do you plan to be a member of when you grow up?"

"Oh, I haven't made up my mind yet. That's the reason Mama Ruth and I go to so many churches. She wants us to become acquainted with them all and when I am old enough I can pick the one I believe in."

Miss Gussie thought this conversation was no less than brilliant, and she repeated it on many occasions. But Jean did join the Baptist Church and she has since transferred her membership to a Houston church. However, she does not take a very active part in church work. I'm afraid that she has a mind of her own; but I've wanted her to have. Again, she's like Mama — independent! As I often say: "How did I spawn a Republican?"

Well, I guess once again the time has come. I've postponed writing this chapter till the very last; and I've put off writing about this theory of mine till the extreme last. The reason for my difficulty is that it is a herculean task. I'm afraid that it's just my conception and not a reality, but I'm going to write it out anyway.

As I see it now, and from a personal and somewhat narrow viewpoint I think the truth is that Minnie—Ruth—and Jean are all basically alike. Oh, of course we have our differences. We were born in various times and have lived under dissimilar circumstances. I wish I had known Mama's ancestors, particularly her Indian ones. Then, I would have more concrete evidence for my speculation. The fact is that I see Minnie—Ruth—Jean as a trilogy; one of those three book affairs that tell three unlike stories about three different people. Yet the three are essentially alike, inherently one, with the mold not having been used before or since. Let it break!

Mama was the strongest of the lot. She was born and reared in a Baptist, Puritanic background, with conventionality as the key note. Yet she dared to rebel against many of the normal taboos. She dared to be herself, to try new things, to be self reliant—regardless of the consequences. She took refuge in sewing and making beautiful quilts, working with flowers, rearing her family, planning innovations in the hotel, serving her community and humanity, and daring to do things that women were not supposed to do. Toward the end of her life she was the victim of old age and infirmities. Yet she plowed her garden only four days before she died. Her spirit passed on.

Ruth is her daughter. I do not know. Right and wrong no longer have clear-cut distinctions. I, too, have had to live somewhat conventionally, being a school teacher in the middle of the twentieth century. My refuge has been in helping the younger members of my family, in travelling to as many places as I could go, and in producing plays and entertainment for thousands of those in my audiences, and for the enrichment and training of hundreds behind the footlights. I had the strange, wild, wonderful break of a few years, first in the service of my country, and second of my incomparable husband for an all too short time, and third of my daughter for as along as we both shall live. I, too, am somewhat slowed down by the vicissitudes

119

of life, but my spirit goes on despite discouragements and impediments.

Jean has lived her more than thirty years a very different life from Mama or from me — yet, essentially the same. Her life has embodied the middle and latter part of the twentieth century — with all its changing customs, morals, viewpoints. Underneath she has been concerned for others, especially for handicapped ones. Although she has broken away from most of the old taboos and restrictions she has, fundamentally, the same qualities as her progenitors. Her outlets have been in her work, her schooling, travel, her students, collecting, pictures, square dancing, bowling, drinking (and I fear me that she does too much of that). She loves her home and her cat, food, reading, friends, possessions, clothes, and she has a magic way with flowers and growing things. It appears at the present writing that she will have no children, but who knows what fate may still have in store for her. But she lives a good life and she has the Minnie-Ruth spirit.

I do not know much about Mama's childhood. I am not certain what feelings she may have harbored for or against her mother. I can only speculate about her disappointment at having to stay home to cook, sew, and keep house for her father and brothers after her mother fell from the surrey and broke her hip. After all, none of us can really look into another's thoughts and feelings.

But I can remember how I hated the signs of old age in Mama, how I dreaded them for myself. I detested her sparse wisps of grey hair rolled on kid curlers so it would lie in soft waves around her face the next day. I can almost feel her lips drawn in a straight, often disapproving tight line, as she criticized my actions. On one occasion I turned abruptly, stalked into the bathroom and locked the door. I grabbed a big bath towel from the rack, and tearing it into pieces threw them to the floor, "There, Minnie, that's better than taking a shotgun from behind the door!"

I loved Mama dearly and tried my best to be a good daughter to her. I have missed her every minute since her death.

But my feelings for her were a strange mixture, a contradiction of each other. *How could I have felt this way?*

Much later, in Wharton and in Houston I have wondered about Jean's feelings toward her mother. Is she, too, an anomaly, a mixture of feelings, a strange hodgepodge of love and hate? She loves me. This I know. She has told me so and she proves it by her actions. She considers me and my likes; she includes me; she tolerates my idiosyncracies; she gives me — oh, so many thoughtful, helpful, suitable, and wonderful gifts — things that will surround me all my life. She has deep sympathy for my age and infirmities. This I know. Her arm is always ready for me to lean on.

Yet, is there a resentment of the difficulties of my age? A sort of nameless dread of the time when she, Jean, will be old and incapacitated. Even as her mother before her felt about her own mother! These things too had been kept hidden. All basically alike — resenting each other yet loving each other at one and the same time. *How could Jean feel this way?*

I have wanted to profit from the example that was set before me. I have not wanted to smother Jean. I have felt that our relationship was close, yes — but that it was sort of special, that we were both tolerant, each of the other, that I was understanding of her way of life. Then I remember the day she got so mad at me that she pounded so hard on the steering wheel of her car that she broke her lovely ring she had bought in the Orient. She told me recently that she had always hated my poor memory for details because she feared that she would get that way too; and lately, it seems that she has. So there are evidences of the same feelings I had about her grandmother. She's such a strange mixture of persons: beautiful — caring for her personal appearance almost too much — yet with the most generous nature of anyone I have ever known. As she says, "Anyone could afford to give a dollar to the Muscular Dystrophy Fund." She tries with all her heart to be a good teacher, to be understanding of her pupils, to make allowances for her friends. She is generous to a fault.

I fear me that our independent natures have taken us too

121

far. None of us has been able to keep the men she loved. Perhaps we were looking for too much. We have succeeded in what we wanted to do, yes; but we've done so alone.

Ah, what can I say? All of us have our individual outlets, yet we are so similar underneath. As Mama held her head high and marched against intolerable odds into the National Hotel, so Ruth and later Jean have to march against difficulties. As Walt Whitman wrote, "We all march to a different drummer." We have all three had infinite love for our mothers, our families, our friends. But I fear this is enough about my theory! The trilogy is yet to be written; but I have misgivings about being the one to write it.

So the National Hotel and its influence lived on in Mama's children and grandchildren. I fear me that it will never die so long as any of their descendants are left living. The strength and dominance of Mama's personality has passed on to her children and her grandchildren, Aye! even so long as any of them are left. What a Breed! What a Legacy!

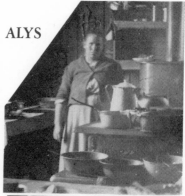

ALYS

AUNT FANNIE

MORGAN

VI

"In some time, His good time, I shall arrive."

— *Robert Browning*

With Emphasis on Minnie Holton Weeden Rucker Called Mrs. Minnie Rucker or Minnie or Mama.

Mama told me later how she had wandered aimlessly about the National Hotel that last night in the spring of 1939. Never had she felt the personality of the hotel more forcefully. The next morning she was to turn over the key to the new owner. Her thirty-five years there were drawing to a close.

I had gone down from Tyler the two preceding weekends and had taken back with me all of the personal possessions that I could — the accumulation of a lifetime! Mama had begged me to destroy most of it; but who was she to advise, she with her numberless boxes of possessions.

The furniture for our little house on Rix Street was all packed and ready to be shipped. In the morning my friend, D.K. Caldwell from Tyler, was to drive her there to live with me. Mama's three children and four grandchildren passed through her mind one by one. Jimmie was planning to stay on in Franklin, secure in her two jobs. Connie and Frances both had their lives settled to suit them. Robert and Lizzie were living in Huntsville. Little Minnie (in her heart Mama still called her that, although everyone else had dropped the diminutive) was happily married; and little Robert was in A&M, so his things were going with her to Tyler. It was decided now — Rain or shine! Sink or swim! Survive or perish! She was leaving the National Hotel and Franklin.

I knew Mama so well that I could imagine the things she thought about on that night. Her mind raced back more than

125

thirty-five years before when she had stood there at the end of the long front porch with her father and her three children; then with her head held high she had marched into the National Hotel. It had been the place of refuge for three families — and an undying influence on many more. It had educated them and given them a good start in life. Mama mused: "Here I am, on the shady side of seventy, saying farewell to the place that has been my home for so long. Alas! Things are not what they used to be. I can see Mr. Silverman sitting there at the domino table; and in retrospect, all the people who have come to the hotel pass in my view. But my business is not what it used to be; neither am I. I know the time has come for me to leave it."

As Mama walked around taking a last look at various things in the hotel, she carried on with her monologue. She had begun to notice that as time went by she had fallen into the habit of talking to herself more and more.

"Ruth says our new home is near the church and that there is a grocery store in the neighborhood. She went there the other day and laid in a nice supply of staples. She bought $7.00 worth at one time. (Imagine how much $7.00 would buy in these days of inflation!) Ruth has lots of friends, and I'll make friends of my own age through the church. Ruth lives such a busy life. I must remember that my purpose is to help and not to hinder her.

"I'm glad I had enough money for the down payment, and all Ruth will have to fork over is the $75.00 monthly payments. I'm doubly glad to have a bathroom and private entrance built on the back of the house. Then I can come and go as I please. And I am overjoyed that Mr. Caldwell has promised to take me to apply for old age assistance next week. Ruth didn't approve of my getting aid, but he did. We agree that the government has this money for people who have been good citizens and have paid taxes. (Remember this was in pre-social security days.) Yes, I'll pay my way all right. I'll not be a financial burden to Ruth.

"The old National Hotel is no more; the new one will have to adapt itself to the changing times. These have been good years though difficult and full of struggle and hardship, mixed tears and smiles. Now, I'll try a new life in the rose capital of America.''

She told me of how she had stood there in the front door irresolutely, fingering the little diamond pin at the neck of her dress. A thrill rushed through her, a sort of stage fright. She caressed the pin as if it were a talisman, symbolizing something special to her. It was not of great monetary value, but it was beautiful and one of the few pieces of really good jewelry that she had ever owned. As she looked in the mirror, she thought about the pictures of her parents and grandparents which were packed in her suitcase. She studied her face carefully and could see that it was clearly visible in all their faces; that she was the latest in a long, unbroken chain dating back to who knows where. But by no means was she the last link; she set her eyes forward and knew that a heritage was still evolving. The ghosts of the past and of the future haunted her, but she was unconscious of the fact that this was a matriarchal inheritance. Minnie herself was the highest point, but her influence and that of the National Hotel would go on to generations yet unborn. The little amulet on her dress glowed with a special luster. It blinked back at her as if to say, ''Come on, Minnie; follow me. Be it good or bad, our influence will shine on in those yet to come. You will make it because you are dominant.''

Mama often spoke to me about the men in her life; she felt that they had failed her somehow: her father, Jim, Henry, Robert; only her grandson, little Robert, had successfully broken that pattern. But she was fundamentally antagonistic to men. She referred to them as ''that fellow'', ''person'', ''boy'', ''guy'', or ''the old man.'' Even though she was an admirable woman she often provoked antipathy in the opposite sex. This quality too has been passed down in one degree or another to all of her daughters, granddaughters, and even great-granddaughters. They have all had to fight tendencies to be too bossy, not to interfere too much in others' lives, to love without smothering. These feelings were mellowed somewhat as life went on. Perhaps they had been caused by the loss of loved ones

127

too soon in life. For, in reality, Mama wanted us to have our chance at happiness; she said as much to me. She coveted happiness for us. Death, with his companions, pain and grief, came to her early; only time was able to assuage the suffering and enable her to accept the finality of a loved one's passing. But she will never forget the waiting in vain for the sound of his horses' hooves as he rode on the trail to Kansas; nor Jimmie for his cheery "Hi, Tex"; nor Ruth for the ringing of the telephone. She has somehow passed on this quality of too much invincibility to her progeny.

Mama spoke about her liking to sell things. "I used to get out and walk all over Franklin selling Gossard foundation garments, cosmetics and hats. They were for sale in my shop in Austin, also. I do not care for social clubs but like organizations with a purpose, such as the WCTU, the Chamber of Commerce, or the Democratic Party. I wish we could go downtown and hear W. Lee O'Daniel and the Light Crust Dough Boys. He is the most dangerous politician we've had in Texas since Jim Ferguson."

This aroused my interest in Pappy O'Daniel and I walked all the way to the public square in Tyler to hear him the next day. The thing that impressed me most was the poor people putting in $1.00, $5.00, and even $10.00 bills into his collection plates.

JoAn came to Tyler to spend a few weeks with Mama while I was away in school one summer. Every Sunday friends came by to take them to Sunday School and church. JoAn remembers one adventure well. "Mammy was distressed because I did not have any white shoes to wear, so one Saturday she declared, 'Where there's a will there's a way!' She and I walked two blocks, caught a bus and rode downtown and stopped right in front of the Red Goose Shoe Store. I'll never forget the pretty white shoes she bought me. I'll tell you, Mammy had a great sense of decorum about what a child should wear."

I could not keep from chuckling when JoAn told me this. The part of the story that struck me was Mama's determination. I recalled one of Morgan's favorite sayings: "I'll tell you, Mrs. Rucker got up this morning with a bee under her coattail."

Mama and I often talked about her religious beliefs. I told her: "You have an essentially religious nature."

She demurred: "But, I didn't go to church much during the years I was raising my family and my son's and daughter's families. It took too much time to make a living for them."

"I think the Lord would understand that, Mama. You grew up in such a strict Baptist family. The church doors were never open without your whole family being there. Your tales about being able to do nothing except read the Bible and Bunyan's *Pilgrim's Progress* on Sunday afternoons are priceless."

"I guess you're right, Ruth. There's a statement in the Good Book, 'Bring up a child in the way he should go, and when he is old, he will not depart from it.' I'm so happy to be able to attend church more and take part in religious activities as I used to in my younger days."

Mama had a very special feeling for those less fortunate than herself. She often fed tramps that came to her back door. In fact, during the depression in the National Hotel there were sometimes more people eating in the kitchen than in the dining room. She swore by all that was good and bad that they left a mark on the house to indicate that it was a good place to stop. But she could not stand for anyone to go hungry as long as she had any food in her house. Mama ended the story, "Occasionally, one of the wayfarers would bring in a few arms full of stove wood or mow a little grass just to show that he wasn't a dead beat."

One of Mama's favorite pursuits was keeping a scrapbook. She encouraged us all to keep one too. Not that I needed any encouragement; my apartment is filled with scrapbooks! Mama was a great clipper, a trait which all of us — especially her daughter Ruth — have pursued. An article in a newspaper about someone in her family usually found its way to her Holy Bible. And the fly leaves were all covered with poems and quotations either pasted in or copied in her own handwriting.

To write a book about her life had increasingly become Mama's desire. To encourage her, I sent her a leather-covered notebook when I lived in Yakima, Washington, and she did write in it frequently. Many bits of information which she had written have served as the basis for things I have written. Later on she sent the book to her niece, Vance, and wrote: "I do hope that you will write the book about your parents and that this will help you. I will never forget my dear Brother Nat and his wife Ella, for they are my dearest ones. If I should die before I get this finished, please send it to Ruth; maybe she will write it sometime." And it was this statement which has spurred me on to get my book finished.

Mama frequently told me stories about her childhood. She recalled: "My grandmother was a full-blooded Cherokee Indian, and her husband was a Frenchman named Prevatt." Oh! how I wish I had listened more closely to the things my mother told me about my ancestors.

She wrote in her book, "I have forgotten lots that I would like to recall. My memory is so short. Yet I can remember things that happened when I was a child far better than much that has happened recently. I have forgotten so much that I would like to remember." Alas! That is my theme song, too.

Mama would not give up. She was as solid as a rock. Her hand closed over her garnet ring, which had been a present from Ruth and was the only other piece of real jewelry she owned. There it was cupped in her palm. In the dying sunlight the stone looked like a drop of blood. It symbolized steadfastness — that throughout her life she should have undying stamina. That's the way Sylvia remembers Mammy, as being absolutely independent. "A woman can just keep on keeping on as if nothing bad had ever happened. Supper had to be prepared. The drummers had to eat. Minnie had to have that dress to wear tonight. Ruth had to get to that play rehearsal. It was compulsory that Robert water his flowers." So the pulse of daily life beat on and held her to the pattern.

Mama could not have functioned if she had not pushed herself to the utmost. And all her children and grandchildren have the same inner drive which they have inherited from Mammy. Jimmie persisted against all pressures. Bob, despite his unlucky star, endeavored to accomplish. Ruth feels driven to do something worthwhile all the time. Connie has to have something to be interested in as an outlet for her energies.

Frances has to push herself to the utmost to do what she enjoys. Minnie seems impelled to press with vigor and effectiveness church, community and personal activities. Jean is determined to have a full and busy life. And Robert, well, Robert is the worst of the lot. He has had the drive to persevere even with the odds of having just one leg.

The girls have all had to fight against this inner drive — even down through the generations; but the trait remains — a predominant characteristic! Mama's great-granddaughter, Sylvia, receives complaints from her husband that she goes as far as she dares, sometimes forgetting that he is the head of the household. Her granddaughter, Jean, even though she is very feminine, sometimes is too bossy for her own good. This quality which permeates all of Mama's female offspring has its tap root in Mrs. Minnie Rucker. She had to keep going. There was literally nothing else to do; and the National Hotel was the vent for her emotions, the means of her escape, her outlet. But Mrs. Minnie Rucker was the focal point. She made it to the top of the mountain. She had endured.

In some ways, I wish I could write that our lives went on happily there in Tyler, but everything was changed by the advent of World War II. Pearl Harbor was bombed and America was soon at war. I got a leave of absence, when I was accepted to be Service Club Hostess in Camp Phillips, Salina, Kansas. We sold our house in Tyler, and Mama returned to Franklin to live with Sister.

Then I was married and went to live in California and Washington. Jean was born and a year later I came back to Texas. Mama had bought the old Hurley house in Franklin and lived there until her death in 1952. She was always plowing away, even to hand plowing her garden the week of her death. She was amazing!

Somehow Mama was ahead of her time. Perhaps her disappointments, her hardships, made her think and act beyond her years. Her successful hotel business was due to a lack in her personal life. She pursued her goals relentlessly. Nothing stopped her. However, I sensed loneliness in Mama. A loneliness that went deeper than I ever heard her admit. Mama was a paradox. In her loneliness, she smiled; in her rigidity, there was a flexibility; in her brusqueness, there was a gentility. All of which I am able to comprehend more easily as the years go by.

Age caught up with Mama. No longer was she able — physically — to do the things she wanted to do; but her mind and her spirit were indomitable. They endured, invincible, like the talisman which glowed on her bosom.

Mama murmured in a barely audible tone:

"I'm dreaming tonight of a place,
The National Hotel by name;
In which we lived and worked,
And which we now proclaim."

"There! Ruth talks so much about poetry that I find myself talking in poetry half the time!"

Yes, Mama could do worse than talk "in poetry", as she put it. But if she did, I think that William Ernest Henly expressed her spirit better than she, herself, could have:

"In the fell clutch of circumstance,
I have not winced nor cried aloud;
Under the bludgeonings of chance,
My head is bloody, but unbowed.

Out of the night which covers me,
Black as the pit from pole to pole,
I thank whatever gods may be,
For my unconquerable soul."